A Language of the Heart:
Therapy Stories that Heal

2nd Edition

D. FRANKLIN SCHULTZ, PH.D.

the Peppertree Press
Sarasota, Florida

Graphic design by Rebecca Barbier.
Cover art by Crowdesigns of New Mexico.

For information regarding permission,
call 941-922-2662 or contact us at our website:
www.peppertreepublishing.com or write to:
the Peppertree Press, LLC.
Attention: Publisher
1269 First Street, Suite 7
Sarasota, Florida 34236

ISBN: 978-1-61493-493-6

Library of Congress Number: 2016919300

Printed December 2016

. . . the noodles I would make for you!

—Italo Calvino, CosmiComics

In memory of my beloved friends and brothers,
Ray and Ken

Contents

FOREWORD

Reading this foreword isn't necessary to understand the material in this book. Clients and students expressed interest in the background for the ideas presented so, I wrote a few more stories. If you find yourself getting bogged down in them, just skip to the introduction and enjoy.

This is a book about the stories we use to describe our lives and make sense of the world. It is about how our personal narratives allow us to be more or less successful at negotiating the emotional terrain of our lives. And, it is about how we can change our narratives to change our lives. It began as handouts written for my clients to help them understand how they came to think and behave the way they do (without overwhelming them with psycho-babble) and to provide them with tools to change their narratives. The ideas behind the stories in this book are based in large degree on object relations/attachment theory while the techniques for change are more cognitive/behavioral.

Traditionally, object relations therapy is very time and cost intensive. Few people have the resources of time and/or money to accomplish the task of a typical analysis. In these days of managed care, there is certainly no financial support for the time necessary to develop the long-term interpersonal relationship of a traditional analysis. Furthermore, there is now a decidedly different atmosphere of belief about what constitutes psychological problems and how they should be addressed. For instance, the narratives of psychodynamics (in general) and object relations (in particular) were, for almost a century, the most powerful explanations of psychological problems. And many forms of therapy were derived from these narratives. However, in recent years there has been a narrative shift from one that defines psychological problems as psychodynamic adjustment issues to one that defines them as medical issues. The medical profession and drug manufacturing companies have developed any number of medications to deal with the symptoms associated with each psychological problem (diagnosis). Clients are often told they have a "chemical imbalance" that is the "cause" of their current symptoms, and they are then condemned to taking medications for the rest of their lives. While attention is sometimes given to psychosocial stressors, there is rarely much consideration given to the enduring patterns of response (that are learned from birth and less than useful), which used to be addressed by psychodynamic narratives (therapy).

This is exemplified by the current treatment of supposed ADHD, where children are given stimulants and the parents are not given any parenting skills training or behavioral interventions that might potentially alleviate the problem. Everybody's happy (except the child) because now they tell themselves they know what the "problem" is. And the child does not get better

— because he's broken. No one has to take responsibility to do anything else because, in this narrative, "He has ADHD."

In all fairness, this is partly due to a need for people to do something to alleviate suffering. We have a need to be active and manipulate "real" things to get the sense that we have done something. So, while the medical doctor actually manipulates neurotransmitter levels with medications, a psychotherapist does not reach into a client's mind with a screwdriver and wrench and make adjustments. I mean, how "real" is an ego? The power and effect of therapy is, thus, ephemeral. It is a "talking cure" produced within the dialogue between client and therapist and not something you can actually see. What's real about that? Curiously enough, talking often works! Though the how and why it works remain to be seen (proven).

But, if talking works, what is actually happening in therapy that has the effect of creating a more flexible response set, or making one more efficient in problem solving, or helping one get one's needs met in a healthy manner? There is an abundance of theories about that. The answer, of course, varies depending on which narrative (theory) of personality you adhere to. And with so many narratives, one can only ask, "Which is the 'Truth?'"

As it turns out, teaching is a wonderful way to learn. It forces you to organize your thoughts and stand back far enough from the topic to gain perspective. A few years ago I began teaching classes in the theories of personality and psychotherapy for students who had returned to graduate school later in their lives. It seemed, at first, an overwhelming task to place the various theorists and ideas in an understandable form for these students, some of whom had experience in closely related professions, but surprisingly little familiarity with the theories on which their professions were based. I had to ask myself many questions. What do I want them to take away from these classes? What will they find meaningful and useful? How do I organize the information so that it doesn't seem like an unconnected list of people with different ideas? The textbooks were useful, though it seemed the students could not find a cohering idea for all that was being discussed.

Shortly into the task, I began using the parable of the several blind men and the elephant[1], who, from their experience, had encountered a piece of reality (the elephant) and attempted to convey it to others. Each, of course, described what he understood about his experience of the elephant from where he stood, but never quite described the essence or whole of the elephant. Notably, it was not only where they stood that was important but also their previous experiences from which they drew their analogies that helped them convey what they had experienced. From this parable, I began to teach the classes with the idea that we were going to try to understand the "elephant" of personality by learning about the pieces of it offered by each theorist. And, to understand how the theories related to the "elephant," we also needed to be aware of the life and circumstances of the important figures associated with each theory.

This idea borrows from Alfred Adler's concept of a "style of life," which suggests that every thing we do and say and the ways in which we organize our lives are a reflection of who we

1 See Appendix A.

4

are inside and what we have experienced. So, we used these biographies as a prism through which to view each theory and to help us appreciate why different individuals focused on different parts of the "elephant" and were partial to different theoretical (logical) frameworks for creating the narrative of their theories. This, of course, assumes there is an "elephant" out there and that there are repeating, discernible patterns (parts of the elephant) that someone might notice and try to describe.

Different theorists sometimes focused on and described the same parts (repeating discernible patterns) of the "elephant" from different angles, suggesting there was a "real elephant" out there somewhere. They also sometimes focused on and described different parts, which others hadn't noticed, suggesting there was more to this "real elephant" than met the eye of a given theorist. Their choice of the parts on which to focus and/ or the descriptions of the parts were often quite apparently related to their own biographical history. And their descriptions of what it would take to change an inefficiently running "elephant" into an efficiently running "elephant" (their theories of psychotherapy, in other words) were also related as much to who they were and how they were raised as to any logically identified connection to a whole "elephant."

So, back to the question, "Which narrative is the 'Truth?"

Well, none of them, actually. The whole truth, that is. What is consistent with each is that it is a "logical" model told through a narrative that explains repeating discernible patterns in ways that make sense to the narrator. This is true whether it be a psychoanalytic, object relations, cognitive behavioral, gestalt, or any other approach to describing personality. What changes in each of these is the story used to explain and understand inner experiences. Interestingly enough, what also changes is the personal narrative of each theorist, and it is the personal narrative of each that both structured what they perceived and how they related it. The degree to which the narrative used captured the experience of the theorist (and others) and could be used to change the response set is the degree to which it was seen as "Truthful." Of course, those who hold to each theory will argue that "the research shows . . ." to make claim to the "Truth" of their theory. What is relevant, however, is not the "Truth" of the narrative so much as it is its efficacy in creating positive change in a less-than-efficiently running "elephant."

If you happen to believe (and I do) that there might be more to psychological problems than a "chemical imbalance," and if you do not believe (and I don't) that medications are likely to solve them, it is probably important to explore how some of these other narratives might be used to address the problems. This book was originally focused on the narrative of object relations. More specifically, on how one might use an object relations narrative in a therapeutic culture that is inhospitable to a more traditional psychoanalytic approach. However, it quickly expanded from just object relations to include other narratives of the "elephant" (attachment theory, behavioral, cognitive/behavioral, etc.) that proved useful. Here, useful is defined as helpful to the practitioner to facilitate change in therapy. It also became clear, in a recursive manner, that it was important to become aware of how narratives themselves structure our perceptions and behaviors. Briefly, it is our own narrative of the world that structures our perceptions. We think in words and make up quasi-logical story lines to make sense of the world. What we say to ourselves (think) becomes our reality. This needs more discussion than would be useful for the scope of this book, so I will leave it at that.

The stories in this book are about how we learn about, understand, describe, experience and traverse the emotional landscapes of our lives. The personal narrative of this landscape (which I refer to as a map) is the story of our lives. The stories in this book are about how our maps may help and/or hinder us in the living of our lives. In this sense they were written for people who wish to stretch and expand their own narratives to more fully participate in their own lives. They are also about how we relate to others, especially about how we are intimate with others. In this sense, they were written as a lexicology, as a study of the language of the heart, and how we can learn to negotiate that perilous territory of love and connection.

The stories are written simply, though the issues are complex. They cover considerable ground. Hopefully, they provide an understanding or way of thinking about how we came to be who we are. They were not written to affix blame (though in some cases it may be well deserved); rather, they are meant to look at process and change and how the patterns of our emotional life were formed. They also look at how we conceptualize and talk about our emotional experience, and what influence this may have on us.

The book is written in two parts, which at first may seem disparate. Part One focuses on individuals and their maps, while Part Two focuses on relationships and couples. They are presented together because negotiating the terrain between being an individual and being connected is a fundamental issue in therapy. The stories in each can be useful in a couple of ways. First, they are narratives I have found effective in helping individuals understand how they came to feel and behave the way they do and what they can do to change it. They are especially useful in facilitating the emergence of an intentional, self-validated individual[2]. Second, they can be used as a primer in developing a personal language of the heart to better negotiate relationships, especially intimate relationships. I will describe a template by which motivated couples can begin to change the ways in which they communicate with each other to facilitate trust and intimacy. There are exercises throughout that provide an opportunity for direct experience of the ideas being discussed.

The stories are hopefully coherent and consistent, the value of which exists in their ability to inform, explain, and foster insight and flexibility of response. It would be presumptuous to assume they were Truth with a capital T. However, if they open pathways to further explore the nature of the psyche, they are valuable. They have proven themselves useful with my clients, who find they help them understand their experience without having to blame someone. They allow them to stand outside themselves and see the process by which their emotional map was created. Many immediately relate their feelings to the stories and thereby find the sense of them. They are not

---

2   This is my favorite description of mental health, brought to you from David Schnarch in *Constructing the Sexual Crucible* and will be discussed in detail later.

particularly original, being the collection of "elephant" stories that they are. Yet, they seem to capture an essence of our being and they resonate within those who hear them. The stories are literally the words I use in therapy with clients to give them a framework on which to hang their experience and, hopefully, a narrative line that is open and subject to revision to facilitate their creating a more useful story of their lives.

The stories have somewhat of an order to them, though when I present them in therapy, I usually present the ones that are most pertinent at the time. That being said, however, I present the stories that are specifically related to an individual's personal experience, self-validation, intentionality and integrity first, even in couples counseling. My work with couples invariably focuses on the individuals first before actually working with their issues as a couple. The reasons for this will become clear as you read the stories. My hope is that you will find reading the stories as useful as my clients have found them hearing them.

ACKNOWLEDGMENTS

As is usual in any undertaking such as this, there are many more who contribute to the final outcome than the one who has his name on it. I would like to thank them all and mention a few in particular.

First and foremost I would like to thank my clients, who taught me every bit as much as I them. I think they would be surprised to hear this. However, as any therapist will tell you, there is an incredible amount of healing that occurs in the therapist in the course of any work with another. For that healing and learning I am very grateful.

And while all of us have many teachers, I have been graced with a wonderful series of mentors in my life. These are individuals who stand out for their dedication to their ideals, their desire to see those around them grow, and the love with which they foster it. These are: my dad, David Schultz, Dr. Donn Baumann, Dr. Kathleen Adams, Dr. Sydnor Sikes, Dr. Jev Sikes and Dr. Eric Gentry. Each of them provided a crucial piece of understanding to my development as a therapist and contributed greatly to the ideas in this book. Thank you.

I also have a family of friends who did more to help me work on my own map than I can recount. They listened to, cajoled, read, laughed at and with, instructed, edited and generally put up with me. Over the course of many years, they taught me how to laugh and sing, and they taught me how to live. These include: Ray, Teresa, Leigh, Larry, Catherine, Andrew, Steve(s), Dave, Deborah and, most especially, Ken, Lou and Dr. Brad. Ken is also my brother, who did the wonderful webpage artwork and book cover design. Lou, a dear friend, did first rate copyedit work to make this work readable. Bradley provided moral, emotional and financial support to make this possible and was a continuous springboard for bouncing these ideas.

Since the 1st edition, the work has grown and begun to take on a life of its own. With that growth have come new friends and new supporters. I would like to add to this list, Lili Parish, whose prodding and persistence resulted in the start of ALOTH workshops and Bobbi Freeman, who both copyedited and helped print the workbook. Thank you all for everything and, mostly, your love.

Thank you all for your kindness.
Sincerely,
Frank

INTRODUCTION

The list of reasons why people come to therapy is really not very long. They are depressed and/or anxious and/or unhappy with their lives and/or in unsatisfying relationships and they have a broken heart. They come in because their lives seem out of control and they feel hopeless that they will ever be able to direct it themselves. This is not to say that each person does not have a unique life and set of circumstances that led to their difficulty. It's just the symptoms that are the same. They often come in hoping the therapist will tell them what to do and will magically fix the problem. Some therapists actually take the bait, stepping in with all the answers with varying, though usually poor, results. There is, however, another, somewhat more Socratic approach that is based in the belief that people have a natural capacity to find their own answers and heal themselves. The therapy stories that follow are based in that belief.

They have a foundation in several theoretical perspectives, such as object relations and attachment theory. This is because much of the discomfort in the human predicament stems from our experiences between the ages of zero and eighteen give or take. We learned patterns of thought and behavior that are less than useful or helpful in our current relationships. Some of the stories describe how we came to think and feel about ourselves and the world the way we do and how we came to behave the way we behave. This is not so we can dwell on the injustices of our past, but to provide us with some traction as we try and understand why we do what we do, here and now, in the present.

To understand the patterns of our behavior, it is helpful to understand their source, because the patterns repeat themselves. A more traditional object-relations-oriented therapy would help us understand the source of our difficulties and hopefully provide us with a "corrective emotional experience" in our relationship with the therapist that would lead to better functioning. However, we do not have to wait until we have had a "corrective emotional experience" to get on with our lives. These stories suggest a solution to the human predicament that is proactive rather that passive — a solution that in concept is simple but in implementation takes some effort on the part of the client. (Alas, there ain't no free lunch.) And the solution is that people become self-validated and intentional and learn to live their lives with integrity.

We learned to be externally validated by the experiences we had in our family of origin, from zero to eighteen. We learned there was a price to pay for the attention (love) we needed; we had to react a certain way or say certain things. As human babies, this probably facilitated attachment and insured our survival. However, in the process of surviving we forgot who we were inside or learned that who we were wasn't good enough. We learned how to interpret behavior and how to react to it to get our needs met. The patterns were predictable and we assembled a response set that was as satisfying as we could manage with what we had to work with. Yet, as adults, the way we learned to interpret behavior and the pattern of behaviors we learned in response to those interpretations often leave us less than capable of managing our lives in a kind and loving and satisfying way. This is because much of our behavior continues to be reaction to the fear of abandonment or being reminded that we aren't quite good enough. The solution is to recognize how that happened (awareness), to remember who we really are, and to overcome the fear - in other words, to take steps to become self-validated and intentional.

Self-validation, intentionality and integrity are the keys to gaining control of our lives and managing the day-to-day stressors that, in the past, have left us depressed and anxious. And self-validation, intentionality and integrity are absolutely essential for creating a relationship with another that is based in love, respect, compassion and true companionship. Without them relationships tend to be mere recreations of past relationships, which were not necessarily that satisfying.

When we become self-validated and intentional, we are able to stand back, look at the pattern and choose to respond a different way instead of reacting the way we always have. In so doing, we become able to speak from the heart and with the heart. In so doing, we become able to love unconditionally. And, in so doing, we become able to do what we have always wanted to do, which is to heal our hearts and be connected with others.

PART ONE

A NEW LANGUAGE

We have this story we tell ourselves, which is the story of our lives. We sometimes tell others parts of the story but mostly it is a personal narrative of who we think we are and what we think we are worth. As you read this section, begin to notice the language you use in this story of your life. Are the words you use kind and thoughtful or are they mean spirited? Do you treat yourself with respect or do you beat yourself up? Do you habitually call yourself names such as stupid, ugly, fat, skinny, clumsy, etc., or use more positive attributes? How do you speak to yourself when you make mistakes? Become especially mindful of the language you use in this narrative. Most of it is used by habit not because it is the Truth. You weren't born thinking bad things about yourself. You learned it. Begin to make an effort to change the language of your narrative to reflect kindness and patience, respect and understanding. Create a new habit of language in your narrative. This will take time and an effort to become conscious of your habits.

The exercises in this book should help you begin to change this narrative of your life. They are intended to help you change the way you think and talk to yourself about yourself and others. As the language of your story changes you will notice that you have a greater understanding and appreciation for your own (and others') experiences. You will notice you begin to treat yourself with the respect and dignity that you deserve. And you will notice you are much less reactive to the words and behaviors of those around you. You will begin to be more self-validated, relying on your own evaluation of yourself rather than what others think and say. You will also gain the ability to choose what you do next instead of just knee-jerk reacting emotionally. In other words, you will be more intentional. Finally, you will begin to recognize how important it is to have integrity, to say what you mean, mean what you say, and do what you say you are going to do, because this is how you will come to evaluate yourself.

What follows are "stories" about how we came to think about ourselves the way we do. They are arranged in a somewhat natural order. However, they may be read alone as complete sections. Clients report they find benefit in reading and re-reading sections as they need them. There are also exercises designed to help you understand the stories in a more personal way. The secret to your success with this book is using the exercises to change the language you use in the story of your life. My suggestion is that you read through the first half of the book entirely and then come back and re-read it, doing the exercises as you go. This is because some of the exercises should be done at the same time and you should know and be aware of them as you proceed.

A note of caution: Just reading the stories may give you some relief, but you will not gain much insight. It takes actually doing the exercises to receive the learning that each contains. There are unique nuances and layers of understanding for you only discovered by doing the exercises. A book such as this would never be able to describe all of these unique understandings. Do the exercises to gain the insight.

MAPS

From birth until about the age of eighteen is when we learn how we think about ourselves. It is when we learn how we think others think about us. It is when we learn how we think couples are supposed to be together, how we think lovers are supposed to be together, and how we think parents and children are supposed to be together. It is when we learn how to deal with anger and sadness, success and failure, joy, disappointment, fear, guilt and all the other significant emotions. What happens from zero to eighteen is that we create a template or map of how the world is supposed to work and how we are supposed to fit in it. Our map contains all of the ways we have learned to interpret behaviors and relationships and all the ways we have learned to respond to those interpretations and behaviors. It is not necessarily the "truth," with a capital "T," of how the world works, but it is certainly the truth of our life as we have experienced it.

We take this map with us out into the world, where the world presents us with its "stuff." As long as the "stuff" the world presents us is fairly well represented in our map, we are able to move through the world, get what we want, life is okay. However, if the world presents us with "stuff" that isn't very well represented in our map, we begin to feel as though we were left out in the woods without a compass. We cannot predict as well what is supposed to happen next and it is difficult to figure out how to actually get what we really want. This usually results in significant, powerful anxiety.

Different people deal with this anxiety in different ways. Some people get drunk or use drugs or food. Others become workaholics. Still others become depressed, have panic attacks or become angry. Some actually become psychotic. As it turns out, all of these behaviors are just different ways people have learned to deal with the anxiety that comes from the fact that their map isn't working so well. These are learned responses created by our past experiences, which led to the formation of our map in the first place.

And this is how maps are created. When we are born, we are genetically programmed to seek attachment to another person. We have to, because as human babies, if we don't attach to someone, we die, quite literally. Before we even have words to speak, we begin to perform behaviors designed to attract the attention of someone who hopefully will come and care for us, want to be with us, and want us to be with them. And if this does not happen successfully or very satisfactorily, what we experience is terror and anxiety. This terror causes us to drop down into survival mode with two options, fight or flight.

This is basically the biological version of what happens to us. Internally and emotionally, what happens is that, from the moment we are born, we feel we have a need to be loved. As children we have the need to have the experience that someone sees us and accepts us and wants to be with us. And if that does not happen, what we feel is fear. This is a powerful feeling, based in the attachment program that motivates us to attend to others for our security. And it is a thread that runs through everything we learn and experience from the day we are born until the day we die.

Now, if that were the only thing we had to learn to overcome in our lives, we would probably be okay. However, it isn't. For instance, shortly after we are born, we are also genetically programmed to look around, explore our environment and seek information. This is another mechanism that helps us learn what we need to survive. In other words, the more you know the better you survive. Imagine how you might feel if, every time you began to just look around and explore your environment, your parents, who loved you so much they constantly worried about your safety, shouted, "Look out!" "Be careful!" or "Don't do that!" It's likely, that eventually, you would begin to associate those feelings of being an explorer with anxiety and displeasure from your parents.

Is this about your parents being abusive? Of course not. In fact, in this instance, it is about their concern for your well-being. While it might be about them not receiving the operating manual when you were born, it is not necessarily about abuse. Nevertheless, all of a sudden there is a space between who you feel like you really are inside and how you feel you have to behave on the outside in order to get that first program met, to be loved by your parents. This is the beginning of how we learn to attend to what others think of us (to be loved) and when we begin to doubt our own internal sense of self. In other words, this is where we begin to learn to be externally validated.

As we grow, there are certain periods in which developmental tasks must be worked through to arrive at an independently thinking, capable, self-validated, intentional sense of self. Each of these periods is negotiated in relation to our parents and their understanding (map) of how the world should work. If we happen to grow up an only child and our parents are overprotective and over-involved and never let us grow into who we are going to be, or if we live in a family with other siblings and perhaps get lost in the shuffle, if we live with parents who must work constantly and have little time to attend to us personally, or if they are particularly inattentive to our internal states and/or have specific, powerful perspectives about what is "right" according to their map, or if we have experienced any form of abuse (physical, emotional, sexual), or if our parents are alcoholics or substance abusers, or if we come from a broken home, or if we have experienced any significant traumatic events growing up — and by now I think I have described just about all of us — by the time we reach eighteen, there is often a fairly big gap between who we feel like we really are inside and how we have learned we have to behave on the outside in order to get that first program met, to be loved.

In fact, by the time we reach the age of eighteen, many of us have come to believe we may never be seen and loved the way we really want to be. And the bad news is that often we blame ourselves. Our experiences have left us convinced there is probably something wrong with us (our "self") and that we are in some way unlovable. Instead of feeling good about ourselves, we feel an inherent shame about who we are inside. And essentially we are left with a broken heart, having the expectation that we will never be seen and loved the way we really want to be and believing it is because there is something wrong with us. We have certainly learned in eighteen years how to hide this piece of information. We hide it from ourselves and we hide it from others. God forbid somebody should remind us of it, because that certainly brings a reaction. But for the most part, we hide it.

Around age eighteen, we leave our family of origin and we take all of this stuff with us. We take the program that says "I need to be loved." We take the program that says "I need to be an individual and explore." We take this map that tells us how to interpret other people's behaviors and what we are supposed to do in response to that interpretation. And we take a broken heart with the expectation that we will probably never be seen the way we really want to be seen and believing this is somehow our own fault.

The first thing that happens is the program that says "I need to be loved" kicks in. So we find an appropriate partner and begin to perform all the behaviors necessary to bring us closer together. We want to be loved and heal our hearts. However, as we get closer to the other person all of the other stuff kicks in. The program that says "I need to be an individual and explore" kicks in and we begin to feel engulfed by the relationship, like we are losing our sense of identity and who we really are. Or we get so close in the relationship we begin to worry our partner is going to see the piece of us that feels not so very lovable and possibly reject us anyway. So, we back peddle a bit to give ourselves some psychological space. We perform behaviors that put distance between the other person and ourselves. Eventually, we begin to feel disconnected and alone, so we peddle forward again performing behaviors meant to help us reconnect and bring us closer together. We find ourselves constantly pulsing back and forth between the need to be really closely connected and the need to have some psychological space and safety.

The problem is that we are in a relationship with someone who is doing exactly the same thing, pulsing back and forth between a need to be connected and a need to be an individual. Only they aren't doing it in the same pulse and rhythm that we are. And here's what happens. About the time we are feeling the need to be connected, they are feeling the need to back up a little bit. Because of our past experiences and our maps, we interpret this behavior as abandonment or rejection. This stimulates that abandonment survival program and we drop down into survival mode, fight or flight. It is likely that, since our childhood, we have learned it feels better to be angry than it does to feel abandoned or alone. So, we react in anger and do something meant to hurt them. They, of course, have to protect themselves and do something to hurt us back. And we find ourselves in a big fight and aren't really sure how it started. Conversely, about the time they feel the need to be connected, we feel like backing up. Because of their map they interpret that behavior as abandoning, reactively get angry, do something to hurt us, etc. You get the picture. We are, many times, left in a rut of unhappy, unfulfilling relationships that seem to veer out of control for no apparent reason.

What's worse is that we seek to have our hearts healed and feel loved and enter into relationships using this map of how we are supposed to behave and how they are supposed to behave. And it is this map that resulted in our having a broken heart in the first place. Because our map contains all of our understanding of how the world works and how we are supposed to behave in relation to the world, we tend to recreate relationships similar to the ones we had in our family of origin. We recreate our maps! We don't do this because this is how we have learned to be loved or because it is particularly satisfying. We do it because it is how we learned to behave in that situation. We do it because, if we don't, we will not be able to predict what is supposed to happen next and we will feel anxious. As we develop, we learn the role we are expected to play. This role is very well scripted and we know all the words in this script by heart. We then unconsciously surround ourselves with people or unconsciously manipulate people who will deliver the cues we need to play out the script we know. Because if we don't, we won't know how we are supposed to respond. It would be like being in a play where we are cued to respond and don't know

23

our lines. This creates a considerable amount of anxiety. This anxiety is so powerful we tend to recreate the same situations over and over even when they are not particularly satisfying. This is why, quite frequently, our lives feel out of control and meaningless. We seem to repeat the same events with the same unsatisfying outcomes over and over. It is why after divorcing, people often seem to marry the same person in a different body.

People have remarkable stamina. They are able to repeat this pattern of dissatisfaction throughout a lifetime, recreating their maps without tiring or ever showing the signs of stress (depression, anxiety, substance abuse, etc.). However, some — in fact, many — eventually wear out, or the stress of their maps not working creates acute psychological symptoms (depression, anxiety, substance abuse, etc.).

And this is the bad news: Though our maps are not particularly effective or satisfying, we recreate them until the psychological strain of doing so creates symptoms (depression, anxiety, substance abuse, etc.) too powerful to ignore. And this is the good news: Though our maps are not particularly effective or satisfying, we recreate them until the symptoms become too powerful to ignore and we begin to look for help! Our symptoms are a message that we need to change the way we think about the world or the way we have learned to behave to get our needs met. In other words, we need to change our maps. And this is also the good news: Our maps are not written in stone. It is possible to change the way we think about ourselves, others, relationships, emotions and the ways we have learned to respond to our interpretations of others' behaviors.

It is not, however, an easy task to change our maps. This is partly because we have a difficult time seeing them. They are mostly unconscious. Just as a fish never thinks about the water he swims in, we never stop to think about why we think the way we think or why we behave the way we behave. We are so intimately connected to our maps and our behaviors have become so reactive, we just do it. If we are to change our maps, we must take them out and look at them. Air them out and decide now, as an adult, whether these "truths" we learned about ourselves and the world as children are really as true and useful as we thought they were. And usually, they aren't. … But how do we take something that is mostly unconscious and make it conscious?

CURIOSITY

This is what I suggest: Be curious! First and foremost, be curious. Be curious about how you came to think the way you think and behave the way you behave. It helps if you are curious without prejudice, either toward yourself or your parents. This is not about blaming your parents or yourself for how things turned out. It is about learning what the circumstances were that left you with certain ways of believing and acting. It is about observing those circumstances from a distance to understand what happened. This is important! Try not to believe that you already know what happened — just be curious.

Here is an aside on belief. There is some interesting published research concerning our tendency to see what we believe. In this study, researchers shined a laser in the eyes of their subjects that reflected back out and allowed the researchers to determine exactly what the subjects were focused on. Then they gave the subjects pictures with absurd images imbedded in them, like placing a flying pig in the clouds over a scene of the countryside. They watched to see how the subjects perceived the absurd objects. By random scanning you would expect people to glance over the absurd objects even if they didn't register them. However, what they found was that people would come to the absurd picture and then go around it. When they came back in a return scan, they would go around it again.

This suggests two things. First, for people to go around something, they must in some way perceive it is there. So the information must be getting into the brain, at least peripherally. Second, they must be going around it for a reason. From discussions with subjects, the researchers concluded the subjects did not expect to see the absurd objects and could not make sense of them. So they unconsciously deleted them! In other words, contrary to the adage that seeing is believing, believing is seeing. We filter out what doesn't meet with our expectations and only see what we expect to see. Curiosity allows new information in, expectations filter it out. This has important implications if you are to become curious about your maps. So let me restate the first paragraph.

Be curious about how you came to think the way you think and behave the way you behave. It helps if you are curious without prejudice (expectations) either toward yourself or your parents. This is not about blaming your parents or yourself for how things turned out. It is about learning what the circumstances were that left you with certain ways of believing and acting. It is about observing those circumstances from a distance to understand what happened. Try not to believe that you already know what happened — just be curious.

The fact of the matter is that you won't find the answer in a day, or a week, or even a month. Understanding the ways in which your map was created will continue to unfold as a process for a long time. You may wish to look briefly over the series of questions in Appendix C to see the kinds of events that led to the creation of your map. Don't spend a lot of time there now, but hold the questions in mind as you continue to read. The subtleties of how your map affects your current behavior and leads to reactive behavior will surprise you. The key word here is reactive. Our behavior is quite often a reflex response to what we have just experienced. For instance, when we are angry, we almost always do things we wish we hadn't done. We act reactively and hurt the people we love the most. We perform behaviors that push away the people we most want to love us. Upon reflection, we think we might have acted hastily. We regret it. We wish we could take it back, but it is too late.

What would it be like if you lived your life with intention as opposed to living it reactively? In other words, what if you chose your behaviors instead of merely reacting to an interpretation of another's behavior? Exploring your map and understanding how you came to believe and behave the way you do is a way to learn how to behave with intention. Living and acting with intention is a crucial concept that we will discuss later. For the time being, just be curious.

ANGER

"Well, how am I supposed to be curious?" you ask. Here is a great clue: Anger! Anger is like a window into your past. And this is why: As it turns out, anger is always the second thing you experience. The first, almost invariably, is abandonment (or, more specifically, the fear caused by it). Whether it is our anger at our children, our spouse, our boss, our friends, our parents or their anger at us, we can unravel it and find a kernel at the bottom that is about how we interpreted a behavior of theirs to mean we were being ignored, treated as if we didn't even exist, disrespected (unloved), about to be left alone (read "abandoned"), or we were reminded of that part of ourselves that feels shamed or broken (read "unlovable"), so, in other words — again — abandoned. Because of the attachment program we were born with, this is perceived as a threat to our survival and we react by entering fight-or-flight survival mode. Then the body prepares itself for battle (anger) or flight (withdrawal). Take some time to become curious about your anger.

An Example:

This is the story of a couple who came to therapy because they were fighting constantly. They had been married for thirty years, had raised three children, and would argue about everything, even the color of the dog dish. They came to therapy because they were no longer certain the relationship was worth being in. Here is some background.

Growing up in his family was like growing up in silence. No one ever spoke. They didn't speak during dinner; they didn't speak when sitting around the family room; they hardly ever spoke to each other at all. However, they did speak when they were angry. In fact, when they were angry, they began by getting very vocal, often yelled and then hit. It was usually pretty clear when they were angry. He felt very alone in his family and assumed the others didn't care much. He told himself that, when he grew up, he wanted a family who communicated more than his, a family who was happy to see him when he walked in the room and who would talk about how they felt.

Sure enough, he married a woman who was very emotionally communicative. She was raised in a family that talked constantly. They talked about their day; they talked about their emotions; they greeted you when you walked through the door; they talked about most everything except – their anger. When they became angry, they initially escalated but then they would shut down, pull away or withdraw. Anger was not an okay thing to talk about or express in her family.

And so this couple married. At the end of the day, she came home and began to talk about all that had happened to her throughout the day and how she felt about all that happened to her throughout the day. She talked about most everything that was on her mind.

And how do you think he responded as she spoke? Well, he didn't respond. He listened quietly. This was partly because he did not have the words to say anything. He quite literally did not have the words to describe his own internal landscape. Nor did he have the language habit that would allow him to respond to her in kind. However, he was not upset with what he was experiencing, and, in fact, he reported feeling pleased in a "family" sort of way.

How do you think she interpreted his behavior? Correct! She had the fantasy that he was angry, because in her family, when you were quiet and withdrawn, it meant you were angry. She interpreted his behaviors as arbitrary and belittling, and she began to escalate her emotional delivery because she was uncertain what had made him angry.

As she began to escalate, he was pretty certain he knew what that meant. He had plenty of experience from his own family. So, he withdrew farther, expecting things to get unpleasant. She would further interpret this as him being angry with her, and, of course, abandonment of her. Her feelings, associated with the fantasy that he was angry and her interpretation of what had happened, spurred her to retaliate by withdrawing. And then he felt abandoned by her. He assumed she was angry because she escalated, though he would not know why. He felt attacked and abandoned by her. Confused and abandoned, he then became angry. He had learned to express his anger.

As he spoke, she interpreted his emotional expression as re-connection. She felt like he was connecting with her and began to calm down. Both were left confused and anxious, having just had a fight and not knowing what it was about. Slowly, their relationship returned to a semblance of stability. This was a pattern that repeated itself throughout their relationship. Never once did they talk about the feelings of confusion and abandonment that occurred during these arguments or process what had happened. Rather, they reacted to their own fantasy and interpretation of what was occurring as filtered (interpreted) by their map. And their relationship constantly revolved around abandonment and anger.

Now you might wonder what kept them together for thirty years given their tendency to argue. As it turns out, having different maps is not necessarily a bad thing. In this instance, their maps were also complementary in important ways. On one hand, his world was a bit cold and unimaginative. He had few words to describe his life and his experience of the world was rather lifeless. She brought color and feeling and liveliness to his life. She, on the other hand, was a little too lively, somewhat uncontrolled in her responses, and constantly embroiled in emotional interactions with others. What he brought to her was stability and a calm center in the storms of her life. This made for a nice complementary fit of their maps and probably contributed to their being together for thirty years.

EXERCISE 1: ANGER

As mentioned previously, anger is like a window into your past. You can use this exercise to help you learn about your past and how you came to think about yourself and others the way you do. Anger is almost always related to the survival routine associated with abandonment. And the behaviors that arise from anger are related to many of the subsequent difficulties you have in your life. When you were younger, you experienced a number of significant events that left you feeling less than loved and protected. These were not necessarily abusive events (although they might have been). They were just events that left you feeling like you had to protect your heart or your sense of self and left you feeling unseen and emotionally abandoned. This is that old survival routine that says if you're not loved, you're in danger and it is related to your need to attach to significant others.

The Anger Exercise is based on the premise that every time you get angry, it is because you are interpreting an event or person's behavior as somehow abandoning of you. This abandonment includes feeling rejected, disrespected, unloved, treated unjustly, or being reminded of your own low self-image (read not lovable). When you interpret events as abandoning, you drop down into survival mode, leaving you the options of fight or flight, anger or withdrawal. It is important to understand that most of the time when you are angry now; you are actually recreating events that you experienced earlier. You have a fantasy that the current event or person's behavior means the same thing you understood it to mean when you experienced similar events, usually as a child. These earlier events caused you to think about yourself in certain ways and respond in certain ways to protect yourself. And these behaviors eventually became habitual responses. Responses, by the way, that are not particularly effective in either keeping you safe or getting your needs and wants met. Yet you continue to do them out of habit.

Performing the Anger Exercise is a way for you to become conscious of the habitual interpretations and responses you use in an effort to protect yourself. As you become conscious of the underlying process, you will begin to notice a consistent language or story you use to explain to yourself what just happened and why you behave in the manner you do. You will also become conscious of the fact that this story really isn't as logical or useful as you might have come to believe. One, the story is rarely the Truth. It is your fantasy. Two, you are not really in physical danger. And three, the behaviors you have been performing don't really work as well as you thought in resolving the situation.

Actions based in anger are always intended to hurt the other person, either directly or indirectly. Anger is always abusive. When you act in anger toward a loved one it is your conscious or unconscious intention to hurt them. And remember, anger is more than just yelling and screaming. It is also disgusted, disgruntled, disappointed, disturbed, frustrated, put off and "I don't care." The "I don't care." is often associated with withdrawal or passive aggressive acts that in some manner are intended to hurt the other person. Anger also manifests as jokes, cutting comments and hurtful remarks said "in jest." If you don't think you ever get angry, ask yourself how many times you have done any of the above. Look underneath the story you tell yourself about "just joking" and own your anger. Then do the exercise.

I recommend you do the exercise every time you get angry, 100% of the time. At first you will be doing it after you've already gotten angry. No matter. You can actually do the exercise on events that occurred days before. The more you do it, the closer to the event you will come. Then, a miracle occurs. The process begins to occur before you act in anger. You will begin to recognize the pattern and, surprisingly, how often it is related to childhood experiences rather than current circumstances. And you will be able to choose to perform other behaviors than angry ones to more successfully get you what you really want.

So, to begin - when you have identified that you are angry, ask yourself the following questions:

1) What just happened that left me feeling abandoned or bad about myself just prior to my anger?

This is an important question because it helps you identify the triggers that create an angry reaction. It is a tricky question, especially if you have not yet realized your anger. Notice your behaviors. If they are hurtful to others or in any way defensive, you are probably angry. Try to identify the exact behaviors that stimulated a thought process in you that includes such words as: "If they would just respect me." "If they just loved me." "Why can't I ever get it right?" "If they would just see it my way." You may even notice that you skip right over this part because it has happened so many times and you simply jump right to: "I'll show them." Or the even less obvious response: "I don't really care what they think." This thought is less obvious because it seems as if you are actually self-validated and not worried about what others say, when in actuality, your feelings are hurt and your behavior changes in such a way as to be hurtful to others. When you are really self-validated, your feelings are not hurt and your behaviors do not change. Try and identify the exact circumstances of the event. Pay close attention to the exact words you use in describing what happened. It often helps to take the time to write out the story. This will give you a better idea of the language you are using and the nuances of the situation to better be able to ask the next question. Then ask:

34

2) How does this situation remind me of similar experiences I had when I was younger?

For the time being, assume there might have been earlier experiences. Sometimes noticing the specific words you are saying to yourself will help remind you of the earlier events. See if you can identify earlier times when you felt left out, rejected, disrespected or hurt in some manner. Or try and identify earlier situations that frequently left you feeling like you would never get it right. Also try and indentify closely similar circumstances to the situation you find yourself angry about. You may have noticed that different people seem to get angry over different things. What angers one person doesn't even matter to another. This is because the situations in which you find yourself angry are specifically related to your personal past experiences. The reason you begin to explore earlier events is to help you identify repeating patterns of experience that, perhaps, left you feeling unloved or unlovable. And there were often words you said to yourself that seemed like the truth at the time. Next ask yourself:

3) Is my interpretation of what they meant by their behaviors or words really the truth about me?

In other words, notice how you interpreted the behaviors and words from the individual(s) in the earlier experience. There is usually an underlying message in your interpretation that you believe them to think you are not good enough, not loveable, will never be loved, can never be loved, or are broken, bad, mean, evil, stupid or uncaring. This was what you learned to think about yourself in earlier experiences. When you stop to think about this message now, as an adult, is it really the truth about who you are? Then ask yourself:

4) Am I in any danger?

Even if others actually think or behave as if I am any of what I interpreted their words and behaviors to mean, "Am I in any real danger?" Remember that anger is just the "fight" part of fight-or-flight. Your defensive reactions are the result of your feeling as if you are abandoned and therefore, not safe. You drop down into survival mode. In reality, there is rarely any real physical danger from the words or behaviors of others. Perhaps there is danger of not being loved or respected, which as a child you interpreted as physically dangerous, but as an adult, there is rarely any real danger. For instance, if someone doesn't agree with you, are you in any danger? Or, if they do not want to be with you or say they do not love you, are you in any danger? Probably not. Nevertheless, it is your habit to interpret these situations as dangerous and drop down into survival mode. Then you perform behaviors that are often less than useful. Finally, ask yourself:

5) Do I have to react in anger or is there another option?

Quite honestly, how often does your angry reaction accomplish your goal of being loved more or respected more? If you are honest, you will probably say "never." So, you have to ask yourself, "Why do I keep doing this?" Your angry reactions are old habits, learned as a child. They may have helped you somewhat then to feel safe, though even that is not very likely. The adrenaline rush we get from anger is often misinterpreted as power but rarely accomplishes what we really want. Will those same habitual angry reactions get you what you really want or are there different behaviors that might be more successful at accomplishing that goal?

It is very important that you try to answer every question the way it is written. The entire process brings the unconscious language of your story to consciousness. Soon you will quickly do them in your head. And soon, the language you use in your story will change as well. Instead of saying things like "He/she made me angry," you will begin to say "Oh, there's that dad stuff" or "There's that school stuff," referring to the event that previously left you feeling unloved. Eventually, you will jump straight to understanding rather than straight to anger. You will recognize that you used to interpret the event as being about not feeling loved and not feeling safe. And now you know you are safe, whether or not you are loved. Here are the questions again:

1. What just happened that left me feeling abandoned or bad about myself just prior to my anger?

2. How does this situation remind me of similar experiences I had when I was younger?

3. Is my interpretation of what they meant by their behaviors or words really the truth about me?

4. Am I in any danger?

5. Do I have to react in anger or is there another option?

SOME PROBLEMS WITH CHANGING YOUR MAP

There are several difficulties related to changing your map. Each of these has its own characteristics that make it particularly important to address. The first five are important for all of us, and so, will be discussed here. There are some other problems that relate more explicitly to specific maps, and they will be discussed later.

First, when you hear these stories, your initial response might be, "But I had a great childhood!" You may become defensive of your parents and the happiness of your upbringing. It is very important to remember that being curious about your maps is not the same thing as saying that your parents were bad or mean or abusive. In some cases this is true and your parents were abusive, but more often they were not. Nevertheless, you learned certain ways of interpreting the world and behaving in relation to others that may not be as useful for connecting with others as they could be. If your relationship history is only marginally satisfactory, if you have been married several times or the one time you were was not so merry, if your relationships with your children leave lots to be desired, or your work experience leaves you wishing you were retired, then it may be that your way of looking at the world (your map) may need adjustment. It is time to become curious about how you learned to think the way you think and behave the way you behave.

Second, if you change your map, your behaviors will change. If your behaviors change, you will not be able to predict as well what will happen next. Because of that, you will feel anxious. This is not just a little anxiety; this is a lot of anxiety. It is the anxiety that has motivated you to recreate your map for years, even though it wasn't particularly satisfying. If you decide to change your map, you have to be prepared to experience some anxiety associated with not quite knowing what is coming next in your life. Knowing in advance that you are going to feel anxious is helpful in the management of it. A useful technique for managing your anxiety will be explained shortly.

Third, you do not live in a vacuum. You live in a system. And in that system you have a role to play. It is a very circumscribed role with a very exact script. You have been in this role using this script most of your life. And the people who are in your life (your system) have expectations that you will continue to perform your role as you always have. If you change your map, your behaviors within the system will begin to change. The system will no longer be able to predict what is supposed to happen next, and the members of the system will become anxious. They will then begin acting, either consciously or unconsciously, in ways that in the past have elicited your old behaviors. As you explore and change your map, it is likely you will need to be prepared for pressure from others to behave as you always have.

SADNESS

Fourth, as you explore how your map was created, you are likely to begin reflecting on things you have managed to push outside of your consciousness for a long while. (Those of you who had a "perfect" childhood are free to skip this part!) You actually begin to feel the sadness or dejection or disappointment or aloneness or abandonment from the experiences you had growing up. And this is what is important to do about that

– nothing!

What you have been doing all along when you become sad is "something." You have been taught since you were a little child that it was not okay to be sad. You were called a "baby" and told to "grow up" or "get over it" to "quit your crying" or (my favorite) told to "quit your crying or I'll give you something to cry about." And so you learned many, many ways to "stuff" your sadness. You deny, cover up, run, distract yourselves, get busy, drink, work, play, get angry, whatever it takes to "stuff" it. And the problem with "stuffing" your sadness is that it does not go away. It piles up. Pretty soon the pile is so big you're afraid if you ever touch it, it will come roaring out and never stop. It will flood you or drown you or leave you dead or dying. And so you "stuff" it.

The "real" truth about sadness is that while it feels as if you will die or be overwhelmed by it, you actually will not. But you have to learn how to be sad. How to be sad without becoming reactive, doing something to "stuff" your sadness. "Why," you ask, "would someone want to do that?" Because sadness is a natural normal emotion. Sadness is always about something you lost: loss of childhood, loss of innocence, loss of relationship, loss of control, and mostly loss of love. Sadness has the unique ability of changing a painful experience of loss into information about what is useful, important, and valuable or about what is not so useful, not so important, and not so valuable. If you stop your sadness from running its course, you just re-stuff it and never really learn the lessons. If you allow ourselves to feel your sadness all the way to the end of it (and there is a beginning, a middle, and an end), it will change the experience into information. In other words, sadness has the ability to change pain into wisdom. And this wisdom will eventually teach you how to love and motivate you to change your own behaviors as you interact with others.

It is kind of like this: You have this story you tell yourself. It is "your" story, about "your" life. It contains all of the experiences you have that you can think about that define you and tell you who you are. You tell others some of the story, but mostly, it is a personal story. When you have painful experiences that you cannot think about because they are too painful and you have not grieved them, the experiences never have an opportunity to take their place in your story. They never have an opportunity to inform you about what is useful, important, and valuable or not so useful, not so important, not so valuable about what you experienced. When you allow yourself to feel the sadness all the way to the end, these experiences get to take their rightful place in your story and you become wiser. And – more loving.

Have you ever tried to sit on a beach ball in a swimming pool, trying to keep the beach ball completely under water? It takes lots of concentration and energy to struggle with the ball, yet it always seems to find its way back to the surface. It takes lots of concentration and energy keeping your sadness from your consciousness, yet it seems to find its way to the surface much too often. What if you let the air out of your beach ball of sadness? Then you could spend that energy doing something you really wanted to do – like feel good about yourself.

This does not mean you will never be sad again. Sadness is

a constantly recurring emotion. In fact, a friend of mine thinks we may be sad as often as ten or fifteen times a day. Usually what we do is work harder, play harder, watch more T.V., drink more, eat more, etc. to distract ourselves. However, when you learn to be sad when it is time to be sad, you then can get on with your life without carrying the burden of that huge ball of sadness. And you will have a lot more energy left over to do the things you really want to do. As you learn to be sad without reacting, you realize how often old sadness and fear from your map has dictated your behaviors.

So, the question is: How do you treat yourself when you are sad? This is a tough question because it is hard to boot-strap ourselves out of habitual ways of thinking. If you have children (even imaginary ones), you might ask: How do I treat my children when they are sad? As it turns out, one of the best things you can do for your children is teach them how to be sad. And, here is how you do that - mostly by doing nothing! When your children are sad you should determine if they are safe and insure their safety. Then, just hold them. Be kind and patient. Tell them they are loved. Do not try to distract them from their sadness, tell them it's okay, tell them it's not important, give them an ice cream cone, tell them to go watch cartoons, or tell them to quit crying. Just be with them. You might acknowledge that they are sad and say that sometimes the world is a sad place. You might tell them that you will be sad with them while they are sad because some-times, you are sad too.

You will likely find this quite a different experience than you are used to both for you and your children. Often when this happens, children begin to open up about what they are feeling. They will tell you amazing little details about what they are worried about or what they have been sad about in the past. And this is what you should do about that – nothing! It is important to simply acknowledge this information. Do not try to fix it. Do not tell them there is nothing to worry about. Just acknowledge it. Your job is to be a witness. And, if you do not react to their sadness by shutting it down, what they will usually do when they are done is get up and go play.

And this is how you can learn to be sad with yourself. Be kind and patient with yourself. Do not listen to those words in the back of your head that say "grow up," "get over it," etc. Just be sad – without performing all of the usual behaviors to distract yourself. And this is what might happen. You may sob. Your tears may fall. Your nose may run. And this may last a day, a week, a month, who knows. You may have weird thoughts come up and odd memories. If you are lucky enough to have a significant other who will just hold you, ask them to not try and do anything to fix it. This might be a problem because others are programmed to shut down your sadness. Nevertheless, ask them not to intervene. Just allow yourself to be sad. Eventually, you will come to the end of it. When you do, you will know it. You will feel strangely empty. And light, as if a five-ton weight had been lifted from your shoulders. And sad. And oddly enough, happy.

EXERCISE 2: Sadness Exercise

The following exercise was not in the first edition of A Language of the Heart. However, since its publication the issue of sadness has come up many times. People recognize almost immediately that their fear of sadness is often the biggest block to their doing the work necessary to change their language and become self-validated and intentional. Surprisingly, the One-point Exercise, presented shortly, is where sadness emerges consistently. Before doing this exercise, you will want to read ahead to learn about managing your emotions. We often manage our emotions by holding our body tight. When you relax your belly and quit holding everything in, emotions begin to emerge. Usually it is the sadness that begins to come out. The Exploring Your Map Exercise, also presented shortly, elicits an extraordinary amount of emotion. And without experience or learning how to be sad, it can seem overwhelming.

This exercise is a little unusual because you are being asked to allow yourself to feel things you have possibly pushed out of your awareness for a long time. If you experienced significant traumatic events in your childhood that are unresolved through personal work and/or therapy, doing this exercise has the potential of eliciting very strong emotions. Monitor yourself. Feeling completely overwhelmed is a good indication that you may need to talk with a trauma specialist or therapist before you do this work.

For this exercise, you are being asked to make the agreement with yourself to not do anything other than sit and be curious. If you need to, just tell yourself this is an experiment to see if there is anything to this Sadness Exercise. You may stop any time you wish, especially if you are feeling overwhelmed. But, while you are doing the exercise, you should not do anything to avoid the feelings other than the One-point Exercise. You should also make the agreement with yourself to not make any decisions about the information you think about. In other words, you may come to conclusions and think you need to go fix something right away. I suggest that you wait before you make any big decisions. When information comes up, just sit with it and let it process. Most of the things that arise will be old stuff. So just let it come up and witness it. Allow yourself to feel the perhaps long forgotten sadness associated with it. This exercise is not meant to affix blame or point fingers. It is a process by which you finally assimilate your past experiences and allow yourself to move forward.

To begin, find a comfortable place to sit where you will not be interrupted for an hour or two. This is very important. Schedule a specific amount of time to do this exercise. Make an agreement with yourself that you will do this exercise for exactly one hour or exactly two hours. You may even want to set a timer. Try to hold fairly exactly to this time frame. You will have plenty of time to do this exercise again. Don't imagine that you will get completely to the bottom of things in one sitting. Scheduling a specific amount of time and not exceeding it is a way for you to control what may at first seem overwhelming. This does not have to overwhelm you. It will, however, be emotional. Also, make sure to plan an additional hour after the exercise to relax. You will probably need this additional relaxation time when you have finished.

If you have a spouse or significant other, explain to them that they do not and, in fact, should not try to do anything to assist you. It is often the case that others around you become very uncomfortable if you allow yourself to be outwardly sad. This is because they are doing everything they can to avoid their own sadness and when they see you being sad, it reminds them of their own sadness. Or, because of their own map experiences, they take your sadness personally and think it is about them. They may try to fix it or help you not be sad even when you have explained to them how important it is not to do that. Try not to let this interfere with your process. If you must do it alone, then do that.

Take some time to relax and breathe. Try to feel your connection to the earth. Give yourself permission to think about whatever comes up and feel whatever emotions arise with those thoughts. Make an agreement with yourself that your intent is to just witness what you have inside, not to "do" anything about it. Your goal is to begin to review your life and identify those experiences that left you feeling bad about yourself or sad. You may find that looking through your Exploring Your Map answers will facilitate this review. Another possibility is to pick a movie you found especially difficult to watch because it made you emotional. Notice especially, those areas where you might initially think you were just angry. Underneath the anger is invariably sadness. Make a space inside yourself for all of the emotions that might arise. Try not to reject any thought or emotion that comes up. Welcome these thoughts and emotions as information about how you came to think about yourself the way you do and how you came to behave to protect your heart. This is not necessarily a pleasant experience at first. It sometimes may feel like a roller coaster out of control. Emotions will well up and come flooding out. Eventually you may find yourself tearful or even sobbing. This is very important: do not judge yourself!! If you are tearful, it does not mean that you are broken, bad, weak, stupid or a baby. The stuff that is coming up is the stuff you have been hiding from your whole life. Be kind and gentle with yourself. Insist that you think of yourself with respect and dignity.

The best thing you can do when these emotions arise is keep your belly soft. Do the One-point Exercise again and again. Breathe slowly and deeply and relax your belly. Remember where you are (in the here and now) at all times. Check that you are "safe." Allow yourself the right to be as sad as you need to be. Don't expect that you will "solve" all of your problems. Just relax and let whatever comes up to come up.

The next step is very important. At the end of your allotted time, stop the exercise. Do not let it extend beyond your agreed upon allotted time. You will always have time to come back and do it again. Take some time to fully ground yourself to the here and now. Take several slow deep breaths. Open your eyes if they are closed, and look around you. Relax your belly. Congratulate yourself for the courageous work you just accomplished. You will probably be somewhat to very tired. This is because you have just done some very difficult work. Take the next hour or so to relax. Treat yourself. Take a nap, or a walk or try a nice bath or shower. Do whatever you like to just wind down. Do not, however, drink alcohol or caffeine or turn on the television. Allow yourself to decompress as slowly and naturally as possible.

Notice the language you are using with yourself. Did you immediately drop back into the old habit of scolding yourself for being weak? It isn't true you know. Relax your belly!! Remember, you gave yourself permission to do this as an experiment. Some people report this to be a very difficult exercise because they are not used to letting go. Not only are they telling themselves it isn't okay, they are reminding themselves of what their friends and loved ones would say if they heard or saw them. This would be a very good time to work on your self-validation. This is your opportunity to let the air out of the beach ball. Your friends and loved ones may not understand that, so how can they have an opinion about what you are doing? You do not have to please them to accomplish this goal. In fact, take this as your first opportunity to be healthy for your own sake rather that someone else's.

Come back to this exercise as often as you like. You may find that you begin to spontaneously start to process sad information. Good!! The object is to keep it flowing through you like water through a hose. You will find that once you give yourself permission to be sad, it will happen more often. However, now when it happens, it will not be painful and objectionable. Sadness is only painful when you clinch and don't let it flow. So relax! We are sad every day. Sometimes very sad, sometimes a little sad. Don't stuff it. Learn what it has to teach you.

**There is only one follow-up question. Ask yourself:
What did I learn about what is important?**

The insights you will get from doing the exercise will come for a significant amount of time after you've done it. You will have "aha!" experiences that seem to just pop into your mind that will help you understand significant pieces of your map and the maps of those around you. Remain curious and keep your belly soft.

LOOKING IN THE MIRROR

There is another difficulty encountered when exploring and changing your map. This difficulty is especially hard to overcome because it is so intimately tied to who you are and how you feel about yourself. As you begin to review how your map was made, you begin to see how you learned to behave to protect your heart. This usually involves reviewing some of the behaviors of which you are not particularly proud. You look in the mirror of your life and find it hard not to be shamed by your own behaviors. You see that you have acted out of anger (abandonment) and reactively hurt people. It is very important that you not turn away from this information.

We have all acted in anger. We have all hurt other people to protect our own hearts. We have all learned behaviors that helped us feel better about ourselves that, on review, we wish we hadn't done. Many of your behaviors are less than useful. If you do not allow yourself the ability to own your behaviors, you are doomed to repeat them. Like sadness, you push out of your consciousness the results of the pain you have caused others. If you cannot think about it, it never has the ability to inform you about what is useful, important and valuable or not so useful, not so important and not so valuable. And, you do not learn and grow from your less than useful behaviors.

Looking in that mirror is often one of the hardest things you will do. It may help to remember this: all the behaviors that you see in yourself and other people that you find less than useful are invariably motivated by a need to feel better about yourself and feel safe and loved. The motives are pure. It's just the behaviors that are less than useful. One way to think of it is like this: Before you learned how to read, were you broken, bad, mean, evil, stupid or uncaring because you could not read? No, you just didn't know how to read yet. And before you learn how to be self-validated and intentional, are you really broken, bad, mean, evil, stupid or uncaring? No, you just haven't learned a better way to get your needs met and feel better about yourself.

Own the consequences of your behavior, both useful and less than useful. And make provision to learn from your less than useful behaviors. As you change your map, your behaviors change. If you take control of your life and begin to live intentionally instead of reactively, you can also live with integrity. Ultimately, you can learn to be self-validated, knowing that you are doing your best and knowing that is good enough. To do so, you must be able to learn from your less than useful behaviors.

GOALS FOR THERAPY

When clients come to see me in therapy, they usually find my practice style quite different from any prior experiences they have had in therapy. Essentially what happens is that I first collect background information and then ask them what they want. I ask specifically what their goals for their life and for therapy are. Then I tell a few of the stories you have already read and give them homework (readings and exercises) to do. In the process of telling stories I explain that I have these additional goals for them. My first goal is that they learn what it means to be self-validated. My second is that they learn what it means to be intentional. And finally, that they learn the importance of living their life with integrity. I believe that when they learn these things, they will know how to manage their life in a healthy and satisfying manner. In fact, my experience is that when they learn these things, most of the problems that brought them to therapy in the first place tend to simply disappear.

So, what does it mean to be self-validated, and why is that important? Being self-validated amounts to rising above the genetic program that has been running your life since the time when you needed it for survival. Remember it? It's the program that says I need to be attached or I will die; the one that translates emotionally as I need to be loved. This genetic program was necessary for your survival at one time, but now fools you into thinking that if you are not attached (loved) you are in danger. Because of your map and how you learned to behave to get this program met, you recreate the relationships and situations of your childhood. And, you continue to believe that what you learned about yourself and others is still the truth of who you are and who they are. But it isn't!

To be self-validated involves two things. First, it means that you remember who you really are. The real truth of who you are is that you were born a delightful, creative, capable little kid (it is my bias that we are born good) who wished more than anything someone would just notice and say, "I love you." Not "I love you, take out the garbage. . ."; not "I love you, get better grades. . ."; not "I love you, let me touch you. . ."; just, "I love you." However, if you are normal, that is probably not what you experienced. Instead, the love you needed was perceived as conditional.

Here's why. As children, there are always expectations: you have to act a certain way, look a certain way, say things a certain way. And if you don't, there are always consequences. As children these consequences amount to either punishment or withdrawal of love, both of which tend to trigger the attachment routine. You become fearful and drop into survival mode, fight or flight. From these experiences you quickly learn you must pay attention to what other people think and say about you to feel good about yourselves. And you learn that you must be with another person or you are not safe. You learn you must please other people or they will leave you. You learn that you never seem to get it quite right. You learn you are not likely to experience what you need the most (unconditional love) from the ones from whom you need it most (your parents). You are left with the feeling that you will never be seen and accepted for who you are. And you are left with a broken heart and believe it is your own fault. In the long run, you begin to forget who you really are.

The second aspect of self-validation is that of managing the fear of abandonment. Imagine what it would be like if you didn't have to react to another person's behavior, behavior that might be interpreted as abandonment (even when they were angry) because you didn't fear being rejected or alone. You would not need to be in a relationship with another person to prove that you were okay. Nor would you need to be in a relationship because you were afraid of being alone, because you would know you were self-sufficient unto yourself. You would be in a relationship because you chose to be with that person not because you needed to be. Not to fear abandonment removes the motivation for most of your reactive behavior because you no longer perceive being alone as a threat to your existence. You no longer drop into survival mode (fight or flight) for protection. As you become more self-validated, your tendency to react in anger will diminish. Events that once seemed important will be less and less relevant to your emotional state.

Here is a question: Why would you, or should you, take upon yourself another person's evaluation of you? Not only is it impossible to please everybody all the time, it is impossible to please the same person across time with the same behaviors, because they are often one way one minute and totally different two minutes later, with different expectations, depending on who they are at that minute. Using another person's evaluation of you and trying to constantly please everyone will drive you crazy.

It's like this. Some people use the number of dollar bills they have in the bank to tell them they are okay. Some use the number of letters they have after their name. Some use the number of friends they can count on their fingers. Some need another person telling them how adorable they are. And almost everyone thinks they absolutely need to be in a relationship to know they are worthwhile. In each of these instances, the way a person is validated is outside of them and provided by the opinion of others. This is external validation. And in each instance, these can change, even disappear, without having done anything different. Then we are left feeling bad about ourselves.

I once saw a client who thought he had it all - money, position, power. He was a businessman and upper management in a well-to-do business. But the economy took a turn for the worse, and his business began to fail. Soon he was out of a job and by now too old to be rehired at his former position in a new company. His bank account shrank and the job he was able to do was far beneath his previous position. From his perspective he was a complete failure. The real truth was that his perspective was primarily the perspective of his father, who held up money and position as the measure of his value. This became a part of him and how he learned to evaluate himself. And, therefore, he was sure of the truth of his failure and worthlessness. He soon became very downhearted and eventually had a "breakdown." He gave up trying.

What he had not paid attention to was the fact that he had changed jobs and even lifestyles in the past and been successful and happy. He did not pay attention to the fact that he was smart and still very capable of living his life with joy and satisfaction. Nor did he attend to the fact that he had a wife and companion who loved him dearly and had been with him for thirty-five years. She continued to love him even though he wasn't an "executive" because he was a "good" man. What he did pay attention to was his supposed failure, and in so doing, became convinced that his life was worthless.

Imagine what it would be like if you really knew at the deepest level that your worth as a person was unquestioned. You would not need others to tell you that you were doing okay. Ultimately, you are the only person who has the ability to have an opinion about your self-worth. To remember your worth as a human and to be your own judge of whether you have lived a life of integrity is what it means to be self-validated.

In short, to be self-validated means 1) you remember who you really are, and 2) you remember that if others do not love you, you aren't in any danger. So there isn't any good reason to drop down into survival mode and be reactive.

THE MYTH OF "I"

So let's talk about intentionality. What does it mean to be intentional instead of reactive? Well, consider the following: When you use the words "I" or "me," you think you are referring to a single entity. This is a myth. There are actually many "I"s inside. There is the "I" that goes to work, and the "I" that goes to school, and the "I" that talks to your children, and the "I" that talks to your mother, and the "I" that makes love to your lover, and the "I" that goes to church, and the "I" that. . . . You get the picture. In fact, there are many more "I"s than that. You think there is only one because you have memory and continuity of consciousness. You smoothly shift from one "I" to the next without realizing that you are really in a different state of being in the world.

These "I"s are called ego-states. Each of them can have its own set of emotions associated with it, its own set of expectations about what is supposed to happen next, and its own set of goals about what it would like to have happen next. Like water forms around a dust particle to make a raindrop, ego-states form around repeated experiences. You have a certain experience in the world — again and again. Over time, a set of emotions, expectations, and goals begin to be associated with that experience. These ego-states may be fully developed and seem like whole personalities, or they may be fragments that are merely feeling-states associated with an event. This is usually how they are developed. However, extreme trauma can also create instant ego-states in a one-trial learning. After an ego-state becomes associated with an event in your environment, your brain takes a short cut. From that point on, when circumstances remind you of the event, out pops the whole package or way of being (ego-state). When an ego-state is elicited, you change the way in which you relate to the world to align with the emotions, expectations and goals of that ego-state.

The problem is, the process is unconscious. You don't stop to think about it. And this is what happens. A certain event occurs and elicits an ego-state that has a specific set of emotions and a specific set of expectations and goals. You head off down the road to accomplish that set of goals. About half way there, another event elicits a different ego-state with a different set of emotions, expectations and goals. Off you go down that road with that set of emotions, expectations, and goals. And then another event elicits another ego-state, and so on. So part of you wants to go this way and part of you wants to go that way and part of you wants to go another way.

The question you have to ask is: "Who's driving this bus?" And the answer is: "Nobody!" For the most part, you are merely being blown around like a leaf in the emotional winds of your life, constantly getting side-tracked by your reactions to events. You switch from one ego-state to the next unconsciously, with little awareness that you are actually in the world in a different way. This is the source of your reactivity and why you seem to have so little control of what happens to you. It isn't until you become conscious of this process that you can become intentional and begin to choose where your life is headed and what you really intend to have for goals.

EXERCISE 3: The Bus Driver Exercise

Throughout the day, you experience shifts in your perspectives and attitudes. Sometimes these are drastic shifts. Sometimes, they are very subtle shifts. If you ever stopped to think about them, it would seem as if you were actually in the world in a different way. You would notice that you now have different expectations, different goals, and often, significantly different emotions than you did only moments ago. These shifts are normal and fairly consistent, usually triggered by some cue in your environment. For instance, notice how different you feel as you walk through the door at work compared to how you feel as you walk through the door at home.

Many, if not most, of your ego-states are habitual patterns of response learned through your experiences from birth until about eighteen years of age. Each of us has many ego-states. In fact, you shift from one to another many times a day. Generally, this occurs without your noticing or being conscious that you shifted. And therein lays the problem. You are rarely conscious of the shift from one ego-state to another. You are triggered and you shift reactively. Sometimes you shift into an ego-state that is less than useful in accomplishing what you want to accomplish. For instance, you may shift into an angry ego-state that explodes and becomes hurtful to others. Or you may have an ego-state triggered that feels like you will never be good enough, so you give up trying.

These are examples of an angry ego-state and an ego-state with low self-esteem. There are many others though, not all of which are angry or feel bad. Some are joyful, some are silly, some feel comforted. Imagine walking into a family dinner on a holiday if you were especially close to your family and had many happy dinners in the past. You might feel safe and welcomed. And sometimes you are in "neutral," where there is no particular way you are in the world that has been triggered by a surrounding event. This, too, is an ego-state, though not necessarily one that was triggered. This ego-state is sometimes confused with, but it is not the same as, the "shut down" ego-state where you are triggered to shut down all of your feelings.

The following exercise is about identifying ego-states. In other words, identifying the different ways you are in the world depending on the situation you are in and the triggers that occurred. Its purpose is to help you become aware of the usually unconscious shifts you make so that you might better be able to choose how you respond instead of just knee-jerk react. It takes some practice and doing it many times to be effective. In fact, attempting to do the exercise may be your first inkling that you are not as in control as you think. Briefly, this is how it works: Take a small card or piece of paper and on one side write[3]:

---

3 See Appendix B

Who's driving the bus?

Stick the card in your pocket or some place where you are likely to run into it at odd moments throughout your day. (At least ten or fifteen times a day is a good start.) This is the first hard part. You have to intend to follow through with the exercise no matter what state you find yourself in when you come across the paper. Whenever you happen to touch the card, see the card, or think about the card, stop what you are doing and proceed with the exercise. Quite likely, you will be in a different ego-state when you run into the card than you were when you made the decision to do the exercise. This current ego-state will not have decided to do the exercise so you will come up with great excuses not to do it. Hmmm! So, who's driving your bus now? If you manage to will yourself through this part, ask yourself the following questions (you may want to write them on the back of your Bus Driver card):

1) What am I feeling right this second?

This is a little difficult at first because you may not be in the habit of paying attention to what you are feeling. You may not even be able to identify feelings right off especially if you are habitually in a "shut down" ego-state. Many of us have been shut off from our emotions and do not have a personal language for them. By completing this exercise over and over again, you will eventually create this language and learn to identify how you are feeling. If you are having trouble finding your feelings, do a quick scan of your body and see if you can feel muscle tension in your stomach or heart or throat. If you can identify tension, for now, call that a feeling and continue with the exercise. Then ask yourself:

2) What in my environment just occurred that elicited this emotion?

Try and identify the exact moment you began having a certain feeling or when you began to shut down. See if it was connected to an event, a behavior from another, or what was just said. Identifying triggers may be difficult at first. They can be as varied as a raised eyebrow, tone of voice, or the time of year. They are sometimes reminders of past events where you had particular difficulty getting your needs met or had to protect yourself. For instance, some individuals have had significant disappointments during Christmas or birthdays. As this time of year comes around there may be a disappointed ego-state waiting in the wings to come out at the slightest sign of the recurring disappointment. However, as mentioned previously, there are many other ego-states, not all of which are angry or feel bad. Some are joyful, some are silly, some feel comforted. And sometimes you are in "neutral," where there is no particular way you are in the world that has been triggered by a surrounding event. This, too, is an ego-state, though not necessarily one that was triggered. As you become more aware of your triggers, you will gain more control of your ego-states. You will be doing the Exploring Your Map Exercise as well so you will probably be better able to identify the triggers. And, in fact, doing this exercise over and over and the Exploring

Your Map Exercise once every couple of weeks will begin to unfold layers of understanding and triggers. Next, ask:

3) How might this be connected to things I experienced or learned about myself from zero to eighteen?

Most of our ego-states are old habits, usually learned before age eighteen. Then we just recreate the same or relatively the same experience over and over. Try to identify the earliest possible time that you noticed a similar chain of events and feelings. You may have difficulty relating the feeling to distant events. While these events probably exist, they may be long forgotten. In this case, see if you can identify what happened as a more current repeating pattern, for instance a similar experience from last week or last month. Eventually, you will remember more of earlier similar events.

If the feelings you are having now are emotionally painful, it is likely there are abandonment issues involved. Be especially mindful of the language you use with yourself. It will change as the ego-states change. Try and identify the words of the message associated with this ego-state. The logic you used to understand the situation at the time was probably the logic of a child. Be sure and put yourself in a child's mind to really understand the message. Your tendency will be to use an adult's perspective and look back as if you were an adult then. But, you weren't. The feelings that you had, the logic you used to understand the situation, and the message you perceived were those of a child. And you based many of your subsequent decisions, understandings and behaviors on that logic. Now ask yourself:

4) Is this really the truth about myself?

During earlier experiences, you might have been told things about yourself such as "You'll never get it right" or other overt messages. However, the messages may not have been specific or overt. You may have just been left feeling and thinking things about yourself like "I'll never be good enough" or "I have to behave this way to be loved and accepted" or "no one will ever really see me for who I am." Ask yourself, now, as an adult, "Is this really the truth about me, or this situation or my life?" In other words, first become conscious of the child's logic and then ask yourself if it's really the truth. It is the process of making this logic conscious that changes it. Then ask:

5) What are my immediate goals?

This ego-state may have a specific goal to protect itself and make it feel better, though the goal may be less specific. For instance, you may notice this ego-state has a specific goal of doing the "right" thing to be loved or accepted like agreeing with what is being said even if you don't believe it. You perform whatever the behavior is you need to perform to get the love you're looking for. If an angry ego-state happens to be out and about, your goal may just be to inflict pain because you feel pain. This is rather non-specific and potentially directed at anyone or anything that crosses your path. The goals of these ego-states are often less than useful, especially when you consider the final question.

At this point do the One-Point Exercise and ask:

6) Is this what I really want? In other words, "Who do I really want driving this bus?"

It is frequently the case that the initial goal of the ego-state that was triggered is short-sighted. How often have you knee-jerk reacted only to regret what you did twenty minutes later? Accomplishing the goal of that ego-state is often less than satisfactory when you consider what you might really want in the long run.

It takes a little practice and the determination to actually do the exercise even when you are too "busy" or too "angry" or too whatever. And there are side effects. Clients often report after doing the exercise for a while they begin to have the eerie experience that someone is watching them. This is a good thing. In fact, the more you do the exercise, the more you will begin to have the effect that you are watching yourself. You will begin to have this concurrent ego-state that watches you as you perform your day-to-day behaviors. This is an ego-state that allows you to stand back and look at what's happening and make long run choices that are usually much more satisfying. From a psychological perspective, this is called creating an "observing" ego.

Another side effect of the exercise is that you will begin to see ego-state shifts in other people. You will begin to notice that others seem one way one minute and another way two minutes later. You may even begin to notice what just occurred in their environment to elicit that ego-state. An example of this is what you may know as button pushing. It is easy to figure out what will set someone off into a tizzy of anger; in other words, identifying something in the environment that will pull out an angry ego-state. Then all you have to do is push their button (create the environment) and - Boom! - an angry ego-state comes roaring out and takes the person on a ride down a road that, upon calm reflection, they wish they had never gone down. By the time they regain some control, it is too late. If it is you with the "button," then ask yourself who is in control, you or the button pusher? And is that ego-state the one you want driving your bus? As an aside, I highly recommend that you not try and elicit others' ego-states intentionally. You already elicit their ego-states merely by interacting with them, just as they do yours. Doing it intentionally will be seen as, and is, manipulation.

It is very important that you work your way completely through all of the questions each time you do the exercise. You may even want to write down the answers to the first few sets. This will give you a more concrete understanding of how the ego-states were created and what happens when each is active. Each of the answers to each of the questions is important. And you have to do them again and again and again. Even if the questions and answers this time are absolutely identical to the questions and answers the last time.

There is, of course a reason for this. You have this voice in the back of your head. It is a constantly running dialogue that tells you who you are, tells you what other peoples' behavior mean and tells you what you are supposed to be doing about it. It isn't the Truth. And you weren't born with this voice. This voice is the language you acquired from the experiences you had from zero to eighteen to help you make sense of the world and be safe and loved the best way you knew how. The problem with this voice is that it has the logic of a six year old – and – it is a habit.

Doing this exercise over and over and over again has the interesting effect of stopping that voice dead. Going completely through the questions will result in your using a different language when you talk to yourself about these experiences. Eventually the voice will take upon itself the language of the exercise rather than the language of your map. In other words, you will replace an old habit with a new one. Changing the language you use is ultimately the goal. When the language changes, you will have a different way of understanding yourself, a different way of understanding others and a much wider array of behaviors to choose from to more successfully get you what you want.

You should begin to notice repeating patterns. As the language changes you may eventually shortcut the process by saying "Oh, there's dad stuff" or "Oh, there's some school stuff," immediately realizing it isn't the truth about you. However, at first, answer each of the questions completely. You may notice that some ego-states habitually lead to others. For instance, an ego-state that involves you feeling very bad about yourself may consistently lead to an ego-state that feels hopeless and acts out by giving up or being angry and striking out at others. Take your time. The lessons unfold in their own manner. Be patient and learn what they have to teach you.

This is the difference between being intentional and being reactive. It is the ability to observe your habitual reactions and thoughts to events and to choose what you do next rather than using a knee-jerk reaction you might have learned early in the making of your map. You become able to stand back to see the larger picture and choose your behaviors to achieve your real goals, not just the goals of a particular ego-state. You respond instead of react. This takes work. Real work. But, it is not impossible.

Here are the questions again:

1. What am I feeling right this second?
2. What in my environment just occurred that elicited this emotion?
3. How might this be connected to things I experienced or learned about myself from zero to eighteen?
4. Is this really the truth about myself?
5. What are my immediate goals?

_____

One-Point Exercise _____

6. Is this what I really want? In other words, "Who do I really want driving this bus?"

EXERCISE 4: A NON-ANXIOUS PRESENCE OR THE ONE-POINT[4] EXERCISE

One of the difficulties with changing your map is learning to manage the anxiety that arises as you begin to behave differently. Being self-validated and intentional means being responsible for your own emotional well-being. It means you must take actions that help you soothe yourselves in the face of strong emotional upheaval, because that is how you remain intentional. This is called maintaining a non-anxious presence.

This task is not easy even in the most ideal conditions because it goes against years of experience and habit in which you merely reacted reflexively without thinking or doing anything to calm yourself. There is actually a physiological reason why you react without thinking when you are upset and this physiological process makes being intentional difficult. The short version of this is that being angry and acting out gives you an adrenalin rush that is (mis)perceived as power and control and shuts down your thinking processes. This is why your actions often end up in results that are less than satisfying. Managing your own emotional well-being is essential to be intentional.

The One-point Exercise is specifically designed to help you create and maintain a non-anxious presence. Performed whenever you are in an anxious moment, it

4   This was an exercise taught by Jim Norman, M.Ed., L.P.C., of the International Traumatology Institute to facilitate the creation and maintenance of a non-anxious presence.

will enable you to think more clearly and respond with intention.

The One-point Exersise is the single most important exercise you will learn in this book!

And, it is one of the easiest ways for you to manage your reactivity and your stress. You may, in fact, think it seems too simple. However, just as there are physiological reasons why you have difficulty thinking when you are upset, there are sound physiological reasons why the One-point Exercise is useful for managing your reactivity. It will probably help you to understand how this works. So, let me briefly explain what happens when you experience anxiety, stress or strong emotion.

THE PHYSIOLOGY OF STRESS

Our brain is layered, with different functions associated with each layer. The middle part of our brain is an old animal part that even primitive animals have to some degree. For you biologists, I am not referring to the mesencephalon, but rather using a broad general categorization for mid-brain substructures. This area is where all of our sensory information goes first. Everything we see and smell and taste and touch and hear passes through the midbrain. This is also where our emotions (sadness, fear, anger, etc.) are located. And, it is where the survival routines (fight or flight) are triggered.

Layered on top of the midbrain is the part most people think of when they think of human brains, with all the squiggly lines running across it. This is called the neo-cortex. The neo-cortex contains functions that make us pretty uniquely human. This is where the language areas are, so it allows us to put words to our experience. It is also where the logic areas are, so it allows us to connect the dots, make sense of experiences and attach meaning to events. And, it contains a function that allows us to manage our emotions.

Under normal circumstances information comes into the midbrain where it is quickly evaluated to determine if we are in danger. If we are not in any danger, the information is sent to the neo-cortex where words are added to it, sense is made of it, and it is stored for future reference as a memory. However, if we perceive danger or we are being overwhelmed by strong emotions, the midbrain triggers the survival routines and begins to prepare the body for fight or flight. This preparation is accomplished by chemical messengers that flood through the body and prepare it to either run really fast or fight really hard in order to survive. You may be familiar with some of these chemicals. They are adrenaline, noradrenaline, aldosterone and cortisol. It is this preparation for survival that is responsible for the experience of the "adrenaline rush."

Here is just a partial list of the things that happen in the body when these chemicals prepare it for survival:

- The digestive process turns off. (There is no need to be wasting energy digesting food when you are running for your life.)

- The immune system is depressed. (Again, a waste of energy if the goal is survival.)

- Blood is pushed from the outer part of the body to the large muscle groups to provide them with energy (oxygen and food) to either fight or flee. (To accomplish this, the heart rate increases and blood pressure increases.)

- Sugar and cholesterol enter the blood to provide energy to the muscles.

If you think about it for a minute, you may find these reactions sound familiar. This is because they all happen to relate to the symptoms of long-term stress. What we call "stress" is really just the physiological experience of the survival sequence being triggered repeatedly. In other words, if the body drops down into survival mode again and again, this sequence of events leads to the symptoms of long-term stress. For instance, when the digestive system is repeatedly compromised, symptoms such as ulcers, irritable bowel syndrome, gastritis, constipation, etc. occur. When the immune system is repeatedly compromised, we end up with all the infectious diseases that come by such as colds and flu. Even cancer and ulcers are now being associated with a compromised immune system. We end up with high blood pressure, high heart rate and high cholesterol. More recent research even suggests that a form of diabetes may also be associated with the constant release of sugar from stress.

There is, however, one more very important event that occurs when we drop down into survival mode. Cortisol floods through the neo-cortex essentially shutting down those functions that make us uniquely human. We lose the ability to think very clearly. We lose the ability to find words to express ourselves very clearly. And, most importantly, we lose the ability to mange our emotions. You have probably seen people who become enraged, turn beet red, and yell an obscenity. This is the process that accounts for such things as "road rage." It occurs partly because their neo-cortex has begun to shut down and they don't have access to the words they need to actually articulate their inner experience or communicate what they want. Nor do they have access to the logic areas or the ability to manage their emotions. When we are in survival mode it is extremely difficult to actually think about what is going on and choose our next response instead of just knee-jerk react. In other words, when our neo-cortex is shut down, it is very difficult to be intentional.

It is a fact, however, that you cannot be stressed and relaxed at the same time. When you are in danger mode, a subsystem of the autonomic nervous system called the sympathetic nervous system is activated. This subsystem is responsible for sending out the chemical messengers, increasing your heart rate and blood pressure, tensing your muscles, making your breathing shallower and shutting down your digestive and immune systems. Conversely, there is another subsystem of the autonomic nervous system called the parasympathetic nervous system, which actually does everything in reverse of the sympathetic nervous system. The parasympathetic nervous system turns off the survival response lowering your heart rate and blood pressure, etc. Intentionally activating the parasympathetic nervous system essentially shuts down the sympathetic nervous system. In other words, you can't be stressed and relaxed at the same time.

Here's an aside.
Did you know that zebras don't get ulcers?[5]

As you just learned, ulcers are frequently one of the symptoms humans experience from unrelenting stress when their mid-brains are constantly triggering the survival response. You would think that being chased across the savannah by a big lion every day would create enough stress over time to cause an ulcer. But, as it turns out, zebras don't get ulcers (yes, they've done the study!). And here's why: After the zebra is done being chased by the lion, he just eats his lunch! In other words, no lion, no stress. A zebra lives in the here and now. Once the lion is gone, his midbrain is no longer preparing his body to survive. Humans on the other hand, remember the lion that chased them this morning and fantasize about the lion that will chase them this afternoon. Many people actually go looking for lions to worry about because feeling like they are in danger and running on adrenaline is what they consider normal. There is never a time when their brain isn't telling them they are in danger. There is never a time when they just "eat their lunch."

5 *Why Zebras Don't Get Ulcers*, Robert M. Sapolsky

And, it is the repeated physical reaction to constantly being in "danger" that results in symptoms like ulcers.

It is the case that your experiences from zero to eighteen including how you learned to interpret what people say and what events mean (in other words, your map), frequently drop you into survival mode. This is almost always about that genetic attachment program. You just knee-jerk react, even when it is a less than useful response. And this reaction is frequently anger, which is just the fight part of fight or flight. You have to ask yourself, "How often has your anger actually gotten you what you wanted?" Most people respond to that question with "never." And then you have to wonder why you keep doing it even when it doesn't work. The answer is because you are not thinking about it. Your neo-cortex has shut down and you are just in survival mode.

The goal of the following exercise is to learn to keep your neo-cortex online, to learn to self-soothe in the face of strong emotion, so you are able to think and choose instead of simply react. It is a means of stimulating the parasympathetic nervous system. Doing it will help you relax and it will help you stay in the here and now. When your body is relaxed, the midbrain no longer delivers the message you are in danger. No lion, no stress. Practice it often, whether you need to or not. The more you practice it the more profound the effect will be.

The ONE-POINT Exercise: A Delightful Two-Step

Step One:

To begin, take a single slow deep breath, in and out. - - When you breathed in, what part of your body moved? If you said your chest, you are probably breathing from the top of your lungs, which, sadly enough is very common. However, when you take a deep breath, your diaphragm should actually drop down and push your belly out of the way. This is the normal way to breathe. For instance, if you watch a baby as it breathes, you will notice the belly rise and fall. But, you have probably been told your whole life to hold that belly in. - - Don't do that! Breathe in slowly and stick your belly out gently as you breathe. Breathe from the top of your lungs and you only move a small percentage of the air from your lungs. Breathe into your belly and you move a vastly higher percentage of the air. By so doing, you put a great deal more oxygen into your blood stream. So, the first step of the exercise is to take a single, slow, deep belly breath.

Now before you proceed to step two, mentally go inside your body. This is a one-time internal check for tension. Start at your head and scan your body all the way to your toes and back again. The object is to notice where you normally hold tension. Don't try and relax it right now, just take an inventory of where you are tense. Some people hold their tension up high and have tight shoulders or neck muscles. Some people hold tension in their chest or arms or stomach.

Some try and push their foot through the floor. For now, just note how your body feels when you are paying attention to your tension.

Next, find the front part of your hipbones that jut out below and to each side of your belly button. Then, notice where your butt bone is (this is the one you sit on). If you stood up, you could imagine lines that run down the front of your body from the level of your hipbones to about the level of your butt bones. Continue the lines back to your butt bones, then up the back to the level of your hipbones and across again to the front where you started. You have created an imaginary box that begins just below your belly button and extends down into your lower torso. Medical professionals call the area of this box, "the pelvic floor." Martial artists, especially those who do a martial art called Aikido, call this area the "one-point" or "center." It is the balance and power point of the body.

Step Two:

Now, take a slow deep breath down into your belly, pushing it out gently as you breathe in. Slowly exhale and as you do, intentionally relax this area called the "one-point." That is, relax all the muscles that begin about three inches below the belly button. - - Okay, now really relax it! - - Let the muscles in the front of your torso become soft enough to touch your backbone. - - What did you notice? If you have successfully relaxed the "one-point," you should notice that you seem to sink down into your chair. Your whole body immediately relaxes, including the parts where you have been holding tension.

At first, some individuals might have difficulty relaxing the muscles below their belly button because this is where they usually hold their stress. If you are one of those people, try doing the exercise like this: Place your index finger on the muscles of your abdomen just below your belly button. As you breathe in, gently push your finger into your belly muscle. As you let the air out, slowly pull your finger away from your belly, releasing the air and relaxing as you release. This will fool the belly muscles into thinking they are relaxed and they will begin to relax. It will take practice.

Taking a deep breath and relaxing your belly accomplishes two things. First, you have additional oxygen in your blood stream from the deep breath and you have relaxed the muscles that control blood flow to your brain. This should result in some of the residual cortisol being flushed from the neo-cortex. Second, intentionally relaxing the belly muscles actually stimulates the parasympathetic nervous system and shuts down the sympathetic nervous system. The fight or flight survival routine shuts down. You can't be stressed and relaxed at the same time. The combination of these two effects helps keep the neo-cortex functioning even when the midbrain is starting to be overwhelmed.

So now, do the exercise again slowly. This time pay close attention to what happens inside your head when you breathe out and relax your one-point. Take a deep breath and relax your belly. Most people report it feels like their thoughts stop briefly, like a clear spot opens up inside their head. Some report that while their head often feels like it is in a vise, when they do this exercise, it feels like tension is being released from the sides of their head out. You might also notice that you seem more clearheaded and better able to concentrate. You may find you can access words a little more easily. It is a very simple exercise: one deep breath and (most important-ly) relaxing your one-point, the belly muscles three inches below your belly button.

Some people find that doing a third step is also helpful. This step involves relaxing your one-point, noticing what happens inside your head and then asking yourself, "Am I safe?" Right this second, "Am I safe?" In other words, "Am I really in danger?" Remember the zebras, "no lions, no stress." It doesn't mean that you won't ever be in danger but, right this second, "Am I safe?" The answer to this question will be crucial as you begin to explore your map and learn to be intentional instead of reactive. This is because your reac-tions were learned in childhood in response to perceiving you were in danger if you were abandoned. You are rarely in danger as an adult. So, ask yourself, "Am I safe?"

You should perform this exercise at least ten or fifteen times a day for the next two weeks. This really isn't such a great number. I mean, it's not like asking you to do ten push-ups ten or fifteen times a day. It only takes a few seconds to take a deep breath, relax your belly and notice what happens inside your head. Take a piece of paper and write "Relax your belly" on it and put it somewhere where you are likely to see it regularly. You can tape it to a computer screen or the visor of your car. Or put it in your pocket. Some clients have been taking a picture of it and making it the back screen of their phone. So that every time they use their phone they do the exercise. Then, whenever you see, touch or think about the paper, do the exercise. Take a slow deep breath, intentionally relax your belly, notice what happens inside your head and ask yourself, "Am I safe?" Pay attention to how your body and mind feel when you are done. You can do this exercise standing up, sitting down, talking on the phone, watching TV, driving your car

What you will notice for the first few days that you do the exercise is that your relaxation level gets deeper and deeper each time you do it. This is because you are training your body to relax on command, which it is not used to doing. After you have done the exercise ten or fifteen times a day for several weeks, something interesting begins to occur. You will find that your body does not like to be stressed and for seemingly no reason you will spontaneously begin to take a deep breath and relax you belly. The relaxation response is becoming second nature. Once this occurs you should notice something else very interesting. When you are feeling anxious or are experiencing a strong emotion such as anger, sadness or fear and you take a slow deep breath and relax your belly, this is what happens. First, you will notice the emotion doesn't just disappear. It doesn't go away. However, all of a sudden you won't have a need to do anything about it. You will notice the emotion and it will feel like it just flows through you like water flows through a hose. And you won't have to do anything. You will find that you are better able to put words to your experience. You are better able to problem solve and think through the experience. And, you are better able to manage your emotions. In other words, you will be able to respond instead of react as if your life were in danger.

This is a very stable place to be. From this position of a relaxed "one-point," you are able to experience powerful emotions such as sadness, fear, anxiety, and anger without having to "do" anything. You have the ability to feel your emotions and you can let them flow through you like water through a hose. This clear space that you create by doing the one-point exercise is the space that Covey[6] calls "the gap between stimulus and response." It is a space that allows you to choose what happens next rather than merely reacting in old, less than useful ways.

This exercise is especially useful when you are doing the Sadness Exercise. Remember that you spend a lot of time hiding from our sadness by distracting yourselves, by drinking and drugging, by being angry, etc. With a relaxed "one-point" you can just witness your sadness without having to do anything. You also have the ability to process angry feelings or intense fear without an uncontrolled ego-state driving off with your bus. In other words, you are in a state where you can decide (consciously intend) what you will do next. Now, if you had to choose an ego-state to drive your bus, wouldn't this be the one you would prefer making decisions about your life?

---

6 Stephen R. Covey, *The Seven Habits of Highly Effective People*, Simon and Schuster Inc. New York

EXERCISE 5: TRIGGERS - EXPLORING YOUR MAP

The exercise Exploring Your Map contains a list of questions identified by others as significant in the development of their maps. These questions are located in Appendix B. They may help you begin to understand how you came to think the way you think about yourself and others and came to behave the way you behave toward yourself and others. In other words, how you became reactive. This is an exercise that unfolds more information each time you do it.

At first, you are not used to thinking about your life in terms of ego-states and triggers. Life just happens. As you explore your map you will begin to realize that you are different under different circumstances and there is usually a trigger that prompts the emergence of that different part of you. Prior to doing these exercises, you were mostly unconscious that you were different. As you do all of these exercises in combination, you will eventually become more aware of yourself in the moment and begin to recognize the triggers or prompts for different ego-states. This is the first step in becoming intentional.

This exercise should be done several times. After you have read the whole book and begun the other exercises, go through this exercise the first time. Be sure you understand the One-point Exercise thoroughly and use it often while completing the answers. You may notice as you go through the first time that some questions seem to jump out at you while others seem to have no significance at all. Pay close attention to the questions that seem important and don't worry about the ones that seem insignificant. Try to answer all the additionally mentioned questions associated with each major question. Take time to especially notice the language you use to explain each circumstance. Be as aware as you can of the story you tell yourself about yourself and about others as you answer the questions.

Two to three weeks after you have completed the questions for the first time come back to them and start over. During those two or three weeks you should have been consistently doing the One-point, Anger, Sadness and Bus Driver exercises. When you begin the questions again, you may find the questions that previously seemed insignificant have now gained importance. This is because you are peeling back layers of understanding about how you came to think the way you do. Most of our maps are very unconscious. We hardly ever stop to think about why we think the way we do, we just do it. Becoming conscious of your map will take time, effort and patience.

There are several things to remember as you do this exercise. First, don't make the mistake of thinking that this exercise is about pointing the finger at your parents or necessarily suggesting that your less-than-useful behaviors stem from abuse. If you have experienced abuse and/or your parents were problematic, the exercise will certainly bring that to mind. Nevertheless, that isn't the purpose of the exercise. The questions cover areas of experience with which most of you have familiarity. These are areas of experience in which you learned to think about yourselves in certain ways and learned to behave in certain ways - ways that may no longer be as useful as they could be for you to accomplish your real goals.

Second, while, in fact, the Exploring Your Map questionnaire is about sixty questions long, these questions really just highlight areas of experience we all have had. There are also several questions you will ask yourself about each of these areas of experience. The specific answer you get to the question on the questionnaire isn't as important as the answers to the additional questions you ask yourself about each question. Two people may have the same answer to the specific question on the questionnaire and have a much different set of answers for the other questions. Again, try to answer all the additionally mentioned questions associated with each major question.

Third, if you are reading this book and doing the exercises as a couple, I will suggest that you do not share the answers you get in this exercise with each other for the time being. Each of you will have certain experiences and certain thoughts and emotions concerning these experiences. When you share them with your partner before they and you are self validated and intentional, there is often a response that causes more reactivity. This is because everybody has an opinion! Due to your maps, ego-states and fear, you will interpret what you hear to mean one thing or another. This is a fantasy! Your interpretation is rarely anywhere close to the truth of what the experience means to the other person. And each of you will have an attitude and opinion about it. If you are still externally validated and reactive you will probably not be satisfied with the conversation you have about it. Sharing your map is a more advanced exercise in the second part of the book.

Fourth, if you experienced significant traumatic events in your childhood that are unresolved through personal work and/or therapy, doing this exercise has the potential of eliciting very strong emotions. This is a warning to monitor yourself. You should not be completely overwhelmed when you do this exercise. You will likely feel such things as sadness, anger, and/or anxiety. However, feeling completely overwhelmed is a good indication that you may need to talk with a trauma specialist or therapist before you do this work. This does not mean that you are broken or weak. It just means that you may have unresolved issues that will be better suited to address with a trained therapist.

You may notice a specific emotional charge to some of the questions. Pay attention to these. It may be that you have ego-states associated with these areas. Ask yourself whether situations in the here and now are similar to past events. Are there cues such as tones of voice, word phrasing, etc., that remind you of past events or feelings? Is there an emotional charge when you experience these cues now that perhaps trigger a reactive ego-state to emerge?

The Exploring Your Map Exercise contains questions about different areas of your early experience. The list of questions is not exhaustive. For each question about an area of experience, ask yourself the following questions as well:

1. What impact did these events have on my way of life, my outlook, my self-image, my sense of safety, my expectations, and my relationships with others?

2. To what degree would I consider the impact to be positive or negative? How so?

3. What are the beliefs about myself that arose because of these events that I might question now?

4. What are the feelings the answers evoke and how do these relate to my current experience of the world?

5. What are the exact words I used to help me organize and understand the events to which they relate?

6. What are the exact triggers that remind me of these events?

Your answers will help you understand how you came to see yourself and understand relationships the way you do.

INTEGRITY

A final goal for clients is that of living with integrity. In this instance, integrity is defined as: saying what you mean, meaning what you say, and doing what you say you are going to do to the best of your ability. This is a particularly difficult goal for many of you for several reasons. First, when you are reactive (one person one minute and somebody completely different two minutes later) you cannot say what you mean and mean what you say because there isn't a single ego-state driving the bus. And second, many of you learned that you will never be good enough anyway, so why try. You learned that you would probably be perceived as a failure no matter what you do. So you learned to hedge and lie and twist and do whatever it takes to be seen in a good light, hoping eventually that you would be perceived as okay. And in so doing, you learned not to be trustworthy in what you say or do.

Here is how that works. When we were children, we really wanted to be loved by our parents. As it turns out, our parents have ego-states as well. Some of their ego-states were kind and loving and some of them were probably less than kind and loving. As children, with which ego-states of our parents do you think we most identified? If you said the not so kind and loving ones, you are probably right. This is because we were already comfortable with the ones that were kind and loving. We didn't have to do anything to get them to love us. The less than kind and loving ones were more problematic. We made an effort to get them to love us. To accomplish that, we took on the characteristics of those ego-states, including the characteristics of their evaluation of us. We internalized this view of us and it became one of our own ego-states. It became the one with which we evaluate ourselves and is usually the one that says we will never be good enough. The question you have to ask yourself is, "Is that who I want driving my bus?"

Here's a question for you. If you tried to accomplish something and did your best and you weren't completely successful, was that good enough? The answer is, of course it was good enough! But, you won't find many who can give you that answer without hedging — well, I can always try harder.

The real truth is you did your best. And, your best is always good enough. Will you perform behaviors that lead to un-expected results? Sure. Will you learn from these behaviors? Hopefully.

The fact of the matter is that you were perfect when you were born. You are perfect right this moment. And you will be perfect two minutes from now when you choose again. Each choice you make for your behaviors is the best choice you can make given the information you have available to achieve the goals of being safe and being loved. You don't always have all the information you need to make an opti-mal choice but you do the best you can with what you have. And each choice you make will have some consequences you like and some you do not like. Notice I didn't say good con-sequences or bad consequences, I said, some consequenc-es you like and some you don't. Consequences are nothing more than information. When you get more information (often as a result of the consequences of your last choice) you will be able to choose again. You may choose to perform the same behavior or you may choose a different behavior depending on the information you get. It won't make any dif-ference because whatever you choose, you will choose per-fectly. You really can't get it wrong. A problem arises when we shift into unconscious ego-states, because any given ego state may not have all the information. Ego-states shift the way you are in the world and shift your understanding of what should happen. As long as you are unconscious of all the consequences you may continue to make the same choic-es without learning.

As you become self-validated and intentional, you are able to use all the information you need to make decisions. Eventually you learn that your integrity is the source of your own evaluation of yourself. You learn to live with integrity because you use it in your own evaluation of yourself, no matter what others think or say about you. You begin to remember who you really are, and you like what you see.

Part 2

A New Language

We have this story we tell ourselves, which is the story of our relationships. Mostly, it is a personal narrative of who we think others are and what we think they are worth. As you read this section, begin to notice the language you use in the story of your relationships. Are the words you use kind and thoughtful or mean spirited? Do you treat your partner or others with respect or do you beat them up? Do you habitually call your partner or others names such as stupid, ugly, fat, skinny, clumsy, etc., or do you use more positive attributes? How do you speak to them when you interpret their behaviors to be less-than-useful.

Become especially mindful of the language you use in these narratives. Most of it is used by habit, not because it is the Truth. Your relationships didn't start with such an angry or negative narrative. You learned it. Begin to make effort to change the language of your narrative to reflect kindness and patience, respect and understanding. Create a new habit of language in your narrative. This will take time and an effort to become conscious of your habits. The exercises in this portion of the book should help you begin to change the narrative and, thus, the nature of your relationships.

LOVE AND CONNECTION

So let's talk about love and connection. This is where the plot thickens. From birth we are genetically programmed to attach to another person. We are hardwired to have and maintain personal contact with others throughout our lives. We are social animals by nature. Why, then, is it so hard to be with this person who we think we love? Why is it that we try so hard for contact and constantly feel empty, hurt and/or misunderstood? It is because negotiating the terrain of intimate emotional connection is a perilous journey for which most of us are ill prepared.

Think about what you have learned about maps. Each of us has a map that is energized by a perceived need for attachment and, especially, the fear of being alone. As we developed, we also were motivated to be differentiated as an individual. Sadly enough, a part of us came to feel shamed and inadequate for reasons previously discussed. And we learned how to protect that part of ourselves we think of as our true and authentic self. We also learned what we could expect from intimate relationships. We learned by watching our parents how people are supposed to act in an intimate relationship. And we learned by experiencing what it was like in our connection with them whether we could expect to be seen for who we are and whether we could trust another not to hurt or reject us.

Each of our maps, organized around the polarities of needing to be attached and needing to be an individual, became the means or pattern by which we learned to relate to others. It is how we learned to interpret others' behaviors and how we learned to behave in response to that interpretation. It would, hopefully, be how we learned to establish that psychological space for ourselves in which we feel connected and differentiated as an individual at the same time, but that is usually not the case. Many of us have never established a balanced space of being connected and being an individual. We came to believe that we had to be in a relationship to be okay and learned that we had to attend to what others wanted to be loved and accepted. But, we did not learn that it was okay to be an individual as well or how to create a relationship in which we could be connected and be an individual at the same time.

This is what we take with us into our relationships, our maps and our perceived needs. And what do our maps tell us to expect in intimate relationships about whether we will get our needs met? How have we learned to love and be close to another (or not) and be an individual at the same time (or not)? What have we learned about whether we can express the things we really feel in trust and safety in relationships?

Of course, the person we "love" also has a map. And their map only slightly matches up with our map. Their interpretations of the world (others' behavior) have only superficial agreement with our interpretations. We make a significant error when we believe they are the same.

This is a fundamental mistake that cannot be too strongly emphasized.

While the maps are superficially similar, they are not the same. And the belief that they are the same is what leads to the many difficulties people experience in their relationships. Their interpretations of our behaviors will be intimately connected to their own experiences of love and connection in their family of origin. Ours will be connected to our family of origin. And their behaviors in response to their interpretations of our behaviors will be those they learned were successful in meeting their own needs of being loved and being an individual or for protecting their own heart in the face of perceived rejection. And ours will be those that we learned.

It is a rare occasion that we enter into relationships with a feeling of safety and trust that we will not be rejected. We often think we trust, but what has really happened is we have negotiated a settlement in which our perceived needs are met (somewhat) and our true self is not threatened (barely) and we have agreed to provide the same for the other person (usually). This, of course, is not done consciously (except for the very perceptive pre-nuptial agreement) because our maps work at the unconscious level, motivating our behavior but not letting us in on why.

As an aside, it is quite likely that we have, in many ways, recreated our original family dynamics, neither because it is or was the most fulfilling, nor because we have the expectation that we will eventually make it work to our benefit. We recreate it because it is what we know. It is what is most familiar. We can predict the results. It is the context that shaped and scripted the role we play and within which we learned to behave. If we do not recreate our usual pattern, we are not on familiar ground. And moving across unmapped territory creates anxiety. Better that we know what will happen — even if it is only marginally satisfactory — than take our chances on worse!

So, we find a person who comes close to meeting our map's criteria for an appropriate partner, "fall in love," and enter into a relationship with them. We have the hope that this relationship will be fulfilling and deep. One that touches our soul and leaves us feeling seen and cherished. One that finally satisfies our need for deep connection. This is the attraction and energy of romance. It is hope and dreams of fulfillment, to finally be loved and accepted. And so often we are sadly disappointed. Maybe not immediately. But often slowly, over time. We cannot seem to make that really deep connection. We cannot seem to make the contact we instinctively yearn for. Our hopes and dreams have proven to be fantasies, and we are left struggling to protect our sense of self.

Many times this experience is met with resignation, sometimes sad, sometimes angry, sometimes hopeless. We hide from it for years. We drink or drug or work or fight or ignore or deny

— whatever way we can — the truth that we have failed in our connection. And some of us have great capacity to live with the knowledge that even though it wasn't a great relationship, it was safe, or it was for the kids, or at least he was a good provider or she was a good mother.

And this, I think, is why we fail to connect: because we learned to be externally validated and have reactive ego-states. Our relationships are often based on the perceived need to be in them and we are unable to communicate what we want and who we are. We have certain expectations that we will never be seen and cherished and, in fact, are likely to be harmed if we show this deepest part of who we are. These are expectations that come from years of yearning for that connection, most especially from significant family members, and not getting it.

We learned how to protect our hearts by never talking about our innermost feelings, our fears, our desires, and our yearnings. We know better than to allow this part of our self free expression because it is subject to the most intense pain, of rejection, of abandonment, and of disdain. It is our most vulnerable spot, which we guard, literally, with our lives. We do not communicate from the heart because, from experience, we have learned it is not safe, and, in fact, have learned there must be something wrong with us. We have been taught to attend to what others think and say about us and tend to believe their evaluation of us. In short, we have become externally validated. We enter into relationships by performing behaviors that will hopefully attract a partner. Because our maps tell us how relationships are supposed to work, we slowly but surely manipulate (unconsciously) our partners into behaving the way we have come to expect partners to behave, while they, of course, are doing the same thing to us.

Here is an example of how our maps work to create our reality through unconscious manipulation:

Because of his map, a man believed that women were untrustworthy. When he and his partner went out, he would get angry if he perceived anyone paying attention to her. Realizing how quickly he would become angry, she eventually changed her behavior when she was out with him to give him no excuse to be angry. She did this even knowing she was not being in any way a flirt or behaving in a less than appropriate manner. When she was not with him she would behave more normally and did not have to imagine how she was being (mis)perceived.

Through subtle changes in her behaviors he picked up that she behaved differently when she was with him than when she was not. This increased his paranoia and confirmed what his map already told him: "Women can't be trusted." His own map/behavior was directly responsible for the development of this situation. The only problem was, his premise and conclusion weren't the Truth.

We have a fantasy of who the other person is based on our own projections of who we want them to be and what our maps tell us to expect of them. They perform behaviors and we interpret them through our maps and evaluate them by how closely they resemble our fantasy. Then we have reactions to that. In other words, we are in relationships with our fantasies rather than real people. We have rarely learned to relate to real people, only our fantasy of them.

We have great difficulty getting past our own defenses, largely because our relationships tend not to be built on communication with another in an atmosphere of trust and safety. But rather, they are mutually agreed upon (though unconscious) ways of behaving (mostly map generated) that marginally satisfy our expectations of what we have come to believe is possible in connection with others. We make unconsciously negotiated contracts in which we are willing to put up with a lot of dissatisfaction as long as we aren't abandoned.

WHAT ABOUT LOVE?

Whew! That is a pretty dim view of relationships. What about love? Good question. Love is a many splendored thing. And, as it turns out, not very pertinent to good relationships. How often do couples report they "love" each other and can't stand to be in the same room together? This is because the word love means different things to different people, even when they think they're talking about the same thing. The emotional experience of love is intimately tied to our emotional learning as children and is, therefore, part of our map.

The exact experience that constitutes "love" for one person is different for another. Excitement, romance, sexual attraction, deep emotional attachment, attachment addiction, wish fulfillment and fantasy are all mixed to varying degrees in the reality of "love" for each person. It is certainly useful for each person to become curious about what the word "love" means to them and determine to what degree that interpretation influences their relationship behaviors. However, "love" is not so important when relationships are failing. Because "love" is not the problem.

The problem is really two problems. One, it is our perceived need to be with another person to tell us that we are okay, and, two, it is a lack of our ability to communicate from the heart in an atmosphere of trust and safety to express what we want to be happy. This occurs because of being externally validated and because of a failure by each person to be trustworthy in the management of his or her own emotions. Put another way, the problem arises because of the lack of a self-validated individual to intentionally treat the other with respect and dignity at all times.

Here is the problem with thinking you "need" to be in a relationship with the person you are with. If you "need" them, you are likely to overlook, ignore, or dismiss important violations of intentionality and integrity. Your partner may reactively get angry because of their map and interpretations. When they are angry they will try and hurt you. Or, they may act reactively and violate your trust by doing something inappropriate. However, because you "need" to be with them and fear if you respond to them they will leave, you will not address these issues. You will stuff them. Or, you will reactively get angry yourself, possibly in a passive aggressive manner. You know by your map how far you can push this so the other person doesn't leave. And you will feel mistrusted, unseen, dissatisfied, angry, disgruntled, and unhappy, but you will not really do anything about it because you fear being rejected or alone.

Imagine, if you can, what a relationship would be like in

which you had no perceived "need" to be in it. You would enter into a relationship with someone because you "wanted" to be with them. Do not confuse the perceived "need" to be with someone with love. This is not love, it is attachment addiction. This is a common mistake that can result in your being with someone who is hurtful and unhealthy for you. It is possible to have a deep emotional connection to someone without "needing" them.

Now imagine a relationship in which you had absolute trust that the other person held your heart safe no matter what. A relationship in which you trusted the other person would always keep your heart's well-being in mind when they acted. Imagine what communication would look like in such a relationship. Imagine what the ability to reveal and discuss the powerful and meaningful experiences of your understanding of the world (your map) would be like. There is more here than meets the eye, so let's explore the dynamics of it.

Keeping another person's heart safe, no matter what, does not mean that you will always agree with them. It doesn't even mean that you will stay with them no matter what. What it means is that you will control your own behaviors to such a degree that you will not hurt the other person out of anger, no matter what happens. Whenever we act out of anger, we always reactively hurt the other person. That angry ego-state comes out and off we go down the road of righteous retribution, or as a friend of mine calls it, putrid retribution. We may reactively mean to hurt them by what we do. Or we may reactively mean to hurt them by not doing something — passive aggression. In either case, it becomes clear that we cannot be trusted to keep them safe. And this is where the rubber meets the road. If we cannot be trusted, we will never be able to break through to a language of the heart.

Unconditional love has the power to heal our hearts. We seek connection. We seek to be seen and not rejected. And by seen, I mean to have someone acknowledge who we are and not feel as if we are being evaluated as bad or broken or unworthy, which is how many of us feel at our core. When we act in anger (which is always a result of our own feelings of abandonment), it is experienced by others as rejection. This is true whether we act angrily toward our mates, our children, our bosses, anyone. It is a message that they are not okay.

And guess how they are likely to respond. Right! Angrily. Because the message to them is that they are being rejected (abandoned). Of course, now they are angry and act in hurtful ways toward us. We then feel more rejected, abandoned, unheard, and unseen, which makes us angrier. You get the picture. Like the couple in the earlier example, all of a sudden you're in a fight, and you don't know why.

There is another side to this issue. As it turns out, the only person's behavior you can really control is your own. When an individual is self-validated, they do not necessarily interpret the other person's behavior as abandoning or accept other's comments and behaviors as an evaluation of their own self-worth. This means that, when a partner becomes reactive and angrily reacts in a hurtful way, a self-validated intentional person does not have to react in anger. In other words, one person can unilaterally stop the cycle of angry reaction/reaction. This does not mean that you put up with abusive behavior. You never, ever have to be abused. It means that you begin to understand another person's behavior as being about their map and their interpretation of the world, not as a comment about your worth.

We may do what we must to insure we are safe and healthy, but we do not have to be angry and abusive in return. When you learn to be self-validated and intentional, you gain access to the control you need to become trustworthy in your relationships and not act in abusive ways. As you become less reactive, your partner will notice, because they no longer have to defend themselves from your reactivity. They will begin to feel safer and start to trust that you will not beat them up emotionally even if they are being reactive. This will in turn result in their being less reactive. They will also begin to be faced with their own reactivity since you are no longer reacting defensively or angrily.

TWO SIDED COIN

This means there are two sides to the coin of improving your ability to communicate with another. The first side is that of managing your own emotions and behaviors by being self-validated. When you are self-validated, you no longer interpret other people's behavior as abandoning, and, even if they appear to be, you no longer fear being alone. So you are less prone to drop into survival mode, fight or flight. You are better able to understand their behaviors in the context of them trying to protect their own heart rather than necessarily being about you. Eventually, this perspective fosters compassion and the desire to seek solutions rather than to attack in anger.

The second side of the coin is that of being intentional. It is making a commitment not to react in anger and cause harm to the other person. You take the time to sort out what happened (by finding your one-point) and respond rather than react. You seek solutions and better communications rather than protecting yourself or seeking revenge.

WORKING WITH COUPLES

When couples come for counseling, I think it is important to find out what they want to accomplish. During the initial interview they usually generalize in some way and say they wish to communicate better and be satisfied. This is then followed by a litany of things the other person is doing wrong.

Stop!

As long as you are pointing the finger away from yourself you are missing the person who has all the responsibility for creating a relationship that looks the way you want it to look. Here is a question for you:

Can you make a commitment in your heart to keep the other person safe from your anger – no matter what?

This is not an easy question, and you don't have to answer right away. However, be aware, the answer to the question likely will determine the outcome of your relationship.

A successful satisfying relationship has trust as the

fundamental, bottom-line building block. The trust we are all seeking is the trust that our heart is seen and held in safety and that our essential self will not be rejected or found inadequate. If you cannot manage your emotions in a way that does not hurt the other person out of anger, you cannot be trusted to not reject and abandon them. If you really intend to improve your relationship, you must start with trust. This is not about you trusting them. It is about you being trustworthy. Ultimately, if you cannot make the commitment to keep the other person's heart safe no matter what (and keep that commitment), your relationship has only a marginal probability of being emotionally satisfying.

When couples come to see me, I usually inform them it is not my goal that they will still be together when they finish! They usually register a bit of a surprise. Of course, I also inform them that neither is it my goal they will be apart when they finish. I go on to explain that my goals for each of them are that they learn what it means to be self-validated and intentional, they learn how important it is to live their lives with integrity, and they learn how to treat each other with respect and dignity. How they choose to behave having learned these things is entirely up to each of them.

This means there are several outcomes from doing this work. First, if neither person learns to be self-validated and intentional, they might either stay married or get divorced. However, if they stay married, it is likely the merry-go-round of arguing and dissatisfaction will continue. If they divorce and marry someone else, it is likely they will marry the same person they are married to now in a different body. Because of our maps, we tend to recreate the same situation over and over.

Second, one person may become self-validated and intentional and, for whatever reason, the other may not. In this situation, the person who has become healthy has a choice to make. Can I live with this or not? This does not always mean the couple separates. In my experience, a considerable amount of change in a relationship can occur even when only one person becomes self-validated and intentional because the healthier partner is less reactive. This can help soothe the other partner who learns they are no longer in danger of being seen as unlovable. They, therefore, become less reactive. A single, self-validated, intentional partner can generate an incredibly healing environment and change the course of the relationship. Nevertheless, as one partner becomes self-validated, they no longer fear being alone. And they may be unwilling to stay in a relationship characterized by the other partner being reactive in an abusive manner. As we explore this further, it will become evident that being able to give up a relationship is often, paradoxically, the key to making it stronger.

Here is an important question, the answer to which draws many emotional responses: If you are in an abusive relationship, do you stay simply because you made a marriage commitment? What if your partner is physically abusing you and refuses to stop? What if your partner is emotionally abusing you and refuses to stop? What are you willing to do to be in the relationship you've always wanted? The point is you never ever have to put up with abuse. And when a person acts in anger, it is my opinion that they are always abusive. At what point do you decide that the abuse is intense enough to give up your marriage regardless of whatever fantasy or religious belief you have about marriage? When you finally decide to walk away, your partner is finally faced with the natural consequences of his or her behavior, losing you. So they must look in the mirror to see if they are willing to accept the consequence of losing you or prefer staying with you and working on their own self-validation and intentionality.

In the final outcome both individuals may learn to be self-validated and intentional. In this instance it is my experience that as each person gets healthier and makes healthier choices, the likelihood their relationship will become stronger increases. The relationship between two healthy people tends to heat up in very positive ways. However, it may be the case that as each becomes healthier they come to realize their relationship is not a good choice for them. They may come to realize they really have different life paths to pursue. In this case, they may choose to separate. And if they choose to separate, it is done in a healthy, growth-promoting way rather than a harmful, destructive way, leaving them loving and supportive of each other.

THE IDEAL PARTNER

When asked, clients describe many different characteristics of their ideal partners. What they boil down to, I think, is this: We want a companion to share this adventure we call our life. We want a companion with whom we can explore passion and ecstasy. And we want someone with whom we can share the inner most pieces of our hearts and trust we will not get beat over the head with them thirty minutes later. While it's nice to have these ideals, the really important question is: are we the kind of person that can supply them to another person? Do we treat our partner with respect and dignity? Do we act with integrity? Are we willing to traverse the territory of connection safely, without hurting the other person out of anger, no matter what? And are we willing to grow? To achieve these ideals takes making an effort to be self-validated and intentional in order to meet the responsibilities of the relationship.

When you are self-validated and intentional you will be less likely to want to continue to be in a relationship with someone who does not treat you with respect and dignity, maintain their integrity, manage their anger or is unwilling to grow. As a self-validated and intentional partner, you will negotiate how you want your relationship to look. (How that negotiation works will be discussed later.) If it doesn't look that way, you may decide to leave. The decision to leave would not be based in anger or fear, but in a healthy respect for yourself and what you deserve in a relationship. The partner who refuses to stop reacting in anger will very shortly have a choice to make. Do they want to be in a relationship with you or not? The point is you never ever have to put up with abuse. And, again, when a person acts in anger, it is my opinion that they are always abusive.

This is usually when the grumbling starts. "But she always . . ." or "He said ..." or "If she would only ..." or "If he hadn't..." The message is: "Fix this person." Said a slightly different way: "This person is not the fantasy I have of them, so they must be broken, bad, mean, evil, stupid or uncaring."

Stop!

Here is a question for you:

Can you make a commitment in your heart to keep your partner safe from your anger – no matter what?

The truth of the matter is the only person's behavior you can control is your own. Do you act out of anger? Why should I trust you, if you do? The question is, what do you want? Do you want a relationship in which you can communicate from the heart? What are you willing to do to get that relationship? Are you willing to make a commitment to act in a trusting manner? Here's the big one. Do you have integrity? Can you make a commitment and keep it?

The very first thing we must do to create a language of the heart with our loved ones is to make a commitment to quit hurting the other person — to become trustworthy. And why is that so difficult? Because, for the most part, we are neither self-validated nor intentional. We seek to be accepted by another and when we perceive (usually mistakenly) that we are being rejected, we react first with abandonment, then with anger. We lash out. We hurt the ones with whom we have the best chance of being seen. So they protect themselves.

The answer to this dilemma is two-sided for each person - that of managing our own feelings and that of not inflicting pain on another. These are intimately connected. The first problem is that of managing our own feelings of abandonment and rejection. In fact, it is our reaction to the other person's behavior that is our side of the problem. We interpret their behavior as abandonment, rejection, etc., which it often becomes after they get angry. Nevertheless, initially, it is our interpretations of their behavior as rejecting that leads us to act out in angry ways. And so, the fight begins.

What if you were already healthy enough to feel pretty good about yourself, to not interpret behaviors as abandoning or rejecting when they aren't, and to not fear being alone when they are? In other words, what if you were self-validated? If you work on becoming self-validated, you will begin to realize that you do not need the opinion of the other person to be okay. Ultimately, you do not need the relationship to feel okay and to be healthy. As each partner begins to realize this, they become less reactive to angry ego-states of their partner's. This leads to less of the second problem: that of reactively hurting them out of abandonment/anger. If you are intentional, and you have made the commitment to not hurt the other person out of anger, you will not react in old ways to start and continue an argument. You will become curious and seek to understand how you came to this place in your relationship.

This is easier said than done because we have habitual patterns of interaction with the ones we love. For couples who have been together for a significant amount of time, the emphasis here is certainly on "habitual." Newer couples are in the process of creating these habitual patterns, which are likely to be re-creations of their maps. It is important to become aware of the habits and to make an effort to circumvent/prevent them.

Here is another question:

Why would you or should you take upon yourself another person's reactivity?

In other words, when someone you are with is having a bad day, why would you want to have a bad day as well? When someone you are with is interpreting the world through their map and being reactive (letting some uncontrolled ego-states drive their bus), why should you also become reactive? Will your reactivity be helpful or hurtful? What do you really want? Do you want to win at the expense of damaging your loved one? Or do you want to find a way to speak about the experiences you have in your heart without starting a battle or losing yourself? And here is that old refrain. When you become self-validated and intentional and make the commitment not to hurt the other out of anger, no matter what, you will have accomplished most of that task. "But how?" you ask.

First, become curious. Begin to explore your own map to learn your potential triggers. Be curious about your partner's map as well. You provide their triggers even if you are not to blame. Approach the task of learning about your map and your partner's map as a journey. Set out upon the journey with anticipation and curiosity but without expectation of what you will find.

This journey is in no way an attempt to spot who is to blame. It is about being curious and fascinated with how convoluted our interpretations of the world are and how they came to be that way. It is about learning what our own contribution is to the outcome and what we might choose to do about it. This cannot be emphasized too much. Each of us contributes to the outcome of our relationships. Each of us has responsibility in changing that outcome. If our own map and our own low self-esteem prevent us from seeing our own contribution to the outcome, we will likely repeat the problem in this relationship and the next and the next. Become curious without blame.

Second, learn to create and maintain a non-anxious presence, even in the middle of a disagreement. This will help you become non-reactive. You can manage your own reactivity by finding and relaxing your one-point, the exercise you learned in Part One to maintain a non-anxious presence. Practice this exercise often. The more you practice the exercise, the more powerful the effect becomes.

The following set of exercises[7] will also help. First, they will help you become aware of what happens internally when you are with another person. Second, they will help you begin to gain control over the reactive nature of what happens. And finally, they will help you create a common ground of experience from which you can generate a new language or narrative to talk about the important internal workings of your heart. They will help you create a language of the heart.

The first few of these exercises were taught as a way to train facilitators to be non-reactive while using the trauma reduction protocol. With slight modifications, they are an excellent means for couples to learn to be non-reactive with each other, especially as you begin to explore the most tender places of

---

7   The first few of these exercises are modifications of a set of exercises developed by Dr. Frank Gerbode and taught by Gerald French in a Traumatic Incident Reduction (TIR) workshop.

your hearts. Do the exercises in the order they are presented the first few times you do them. They are intended to allow you to maintain a progressively non-anxious presence in more and more reactive situations. They will also help you become aware of how your own map and expectations intrude on and interfere with communications between you and your partner.

It is useful, though not absolutely necessary, to do these exercises with a partner with whom you are in a relationship, because as you progress, you can come to trust they will not be reactive. In many instances, however, you can do the exercises unilaterally with others. In other words, do them mentally to yourself when you are with others. The exercises will help you recognize how often your own external validation and reactivity interfere with your ability to communicate with others. The goal of the exercises, when done with a significant other, is to create a partner and companion in this adventure called your life, instead of creating a reactive adversary. They lay the groundwork necessary for creating a language of the heart with which you can speak from the heart and to another's heart without fear that you will be misinterpreted, reacted negatively toward, or judged as broken, bad, mean, evil, stupid or uncaring. However, our reactivity comes from our own fear of abandonment. When we are self-validated, we are less reactive because we do not interpret others' behavior as abandoning or as a comment about our self worth. So, the first few exercises focus on your own reactivity. Later exercises begin the more arduous journey of traversing the territory of connection to another with safety and love.

Some people report the exercises seem stilted and

over-structured. There is a reason for this. They push you into areas of experience you would not normally enter. They are uncomfortable, at first, because it is new territory and anxiety provoking. As you progress, you will become more comfortable both feeling and expressing your feelings with a partner. The structure will help you feel more secure until you are able to traverse the territory and manage your anxiety at the same time. Again the caveat, there "ain't no free lunch." You actually have to do the exercises to benefit from them. Reading about them is not enough. So, take a deep breath, relax your one-point and begin.

EXERCISE 6: AWARENESS

Position yourselves so that you are just barely inside each other's personal space, approximately knee to knee, facing each other, without touching. Find and relax your one-point. Close your eyes. Your goal is to be mentally present and aware of your partner. Nothing else! If thoughts emerge, acknowledge them and return to being present and aware. Continue as long as possible. Be curious about what happens.

Notice the goal is to be mentally present and aware of your partner and nothing else. Some people have great difficulty being present. As soon as their eyes close, their mind opens. They wiggle. They fidget. They have one association after another and have little ability to focus on the here and now, let alone be aware of their partner. Be curious about those associations. What makes you react and pull your attention away from your partner? Notice how often you revert to a fantasy about what you are doing rather than actually doing it. Or notice the line of thought. It often gives clues to your own map and your own interpretations. This is underlying noise in your communication with the other person.

Some people have difficulty being aware of the other person. "How can I be aware with my eyes closed?" as if the eyes were the only sense. "I just have to create a picture of them to be aware of them." as if there were no reality to the person other than the image of them. "What am I supposed to be aware of?" as if there were a particular thing one had to be aware of. "What am I supposed to be doing?" as if there were something one was supposed to do with information they become aware of. In this exercise, your goal is to simply be aware. You don't have to do anything with what you become aware of. Curiosity helps. To do the exercise, you should create an attitude of curious awareness, without the need to do anything with the information you obtain. Again, notice how much fantasy intrudes on the exercise. Often we immediately assume there must be something about the other person that makes the exercise difficult. Or we are distracted and claim that a sound or a light drew our attention away. In truth, we can focus our attention with intention. If it is drawn away, it is because we are being reactive. Be curious about the nature and source of your reactivity.

Frequently, emotions emerge - fear, anxiety, anger, sadness. Be especially curious about these. There is nothing in the exercise that should elicit emotions. So, if they emerge, there is something about your interpretation of the experience that is related to the emotions. You are having a fantasy about what the exercise means and then, having an emotional response to your fantasy. This is the nature and pattern of many of the responses in a relationship if we are not intentional. First we have a fantasy about the meaning of the event and then we have an emotion associated with the fantasy we're having - out pops an ego-state and down the road we go. Continue this exercise until you are fairly well able to be present and aware for at least 5 minutes.

One caveat: if you and your partner decide to discuss your experiences, remember that it is possible you are still reactive. You have not yet learned to hear what the other has to say without having a fantasy about what their comments mean and reacting to it. If your discussion follows previous predictable lines and this is not where you want to go, stop the external discussion and continue the exercises with internal discussion (personal revelations) only.

Here are some questions you can ask yourself about this experience:

1. Were there any immediate difficulties settling into the exercise? What, if anything, were you distracted by?

2. Did any emotions arise? As you think about them now, to what part of your map are they related? What was the trigger?

3. Did any particular fantasies arise related to this exercise, either about your partner or the exercise itself?

4. Was there an identifiable ego-state triggered?

EXERCISE 7: MORE AWARENESS

This exercise is exactly the same as Exercise 6, only done with your eyes open! Eyes open presents a special challenge because we have habitual patterns of contact avoidance we use when we interact with others. Find your partner's dominant eye, which if you look back and forth during the initial instants of the exercise, you should be easily able to identify. Once you find it, softly focus on that eye with intentional attention. Do not continue to scan back and forth or find a point somewhere between the two and focus there. Gaze into their dominant eye. Find your one-point and relax. Be present and aware and nothing else. If thoughts emerge, acknowledge them and release them. Be curious about what happens.

Again, notice the fantasies, emotions and thoughts that emerge and distract you. The exercise itself is without content, yet your mind takes you on a journey by attaching meaning to insignificant events. Again, we have a fantasy about the meaning of the event and then we have an emotion associated with the fantasy we're having, then out pops an ego-state, etc. Continue this exercise until you are fairly well able to be present and aware for at least 5 minutes.

Again, here are some questions you can ask yourself about this experience:

1. Were there any immediate difficulties settling into the exercise? What, if anything, were you distracted by?

2. Did any emotions arise? As you think about them now, to what part of your map are they related? What was the trigger?

3. Did any particular fantasies arise related to this exercise, either about your partner or the exercise itself?

4. Was there an identifiable ego-state triggered?

EXERCISE 8: REACTIVITY

For this exercise, you and your partner will take turns being a coach or trainer and a trainee. It is set up in the same manner as the previous exercises. So, position yourselves so that you are just barely inside each other's personal space, approximately knee to knee, facing each other, without touching. In this exercise, it will be the job of the coach to attempt to get the trainee to smile or react in some way. The trainee's job is to remain curiously attentive without reacting. In other words, the trainee should be present and attentive and remain non-reactive.

The coach should use a movement or facial expression or word (trigger) that elicits laughter or other reaction from the trainee. When the trainee reacts, stop the exercise. Use a time out signal to indicate you are stopping the exercise. Give the trainee a moment to find their one-point and relax and begin again. When the trainee is ready to resume, s/he should say, "Begin." Repeat exactly the same movement, facial expression, or word (trigger) that elicited the reaction the first time.

Continue in this manner until the trainee is no longer reactive to that trigger.

Change roles. Repeat this process several times.

Notice how laughter and/or emotions and thoughts well up in the trainee. These reactions demonstrate their attention is not intentional. However, with practice, attention can become very intentional, where it is your intent to remain curiously attentive without reacting.

Some individuals find this exercise very difficult at first; though most quickly learn to be non-reactive. Be curious about the emotions and thoughts that arise. These are triggered by the trainee's map, interpretation and fantasy of the meaning of the coach's behavior. Imagine how many triggers you might have if the coach was yelling or saying things in anger.

In due course, the goal is to become non-reactive in the face of an angry partner. Remember, anger is always the second emotion. It is about the individual interpreting a comment or behavior as abandoning, and it is not necessarily the truth. As a partner, why would you or should you become reactive to your partner's map, interpretation and/or reaction?

When you are self-validated and intentional and living with integrity, you will be able to be aware of your partner's anger and reactivity without becoming angry in defense, because you will know your intent was not to abandon or cause pain. This means their reaction is about their own map and interpretation of behavior. By not reacting, you circumvent an argument about something that usually has nothing to do with the reason each of you is so reactive. You also give your partner time to regain their one-point to better articulate their experience.

Eventually you will be able to hear and discuss the most intimate details of the other person's heart without becoming emotionally reactive, allowing them to say what they feel without interpreting it as abandoning and hurtful of you and allowing you both to begin to traverse that perilous territory of connection safely.

Again, here are some questions you can ask yourself about this experience:

1. Were there any immediate difficulties settling into the exercise? What, if anything, were you distracted by?

2. Did any emotions arise? As you think about them now, to what part of your map are they related? What was the trigger?

3. Did any particular fantasies arise related to this exercise, either about your partner or the exercise itself?

4. Was there an identifiable ego-state triggered?

EXERCISE 9: ACKNOWLEDGMENT

This is a brief exercise but important nonetheless. In this exercise the goal is to insure the person communicating has been acknowledged. This doesn't necessarily mean that the person doing the acknowledging agrees with the person communicating. It is just a means to indicate the message has been received.

Frequently when couples communicate, they repeat what they have tried to communicate again and again because there has been insufficient acknowledgement that the communication has been received. When communications are not acknowledged, the message to the communicator is that their communication is unimportant, leading rapidly to feelings of being ignored or slighted and, of course, abandoned. This frequently leads to escalation to an argument.

This is also an opportunity for the trainee to practice being non-reactive, present, and aware in the here and now without adding any interpretations or inner reactions. While this exercise uses relatively innocuous statements from the coach, later exercises will use more emotionally laden statements that, in the past, have caused reactivity in the listener.

This exercise, again, has a coach and a trainee. In this instance, the coach is the communicator and the trainee is the acknowledger. The coach will, in advance, create a short list of innocuous statements that will be communicated to the trainee. The list should contain non-emotion laden statements such as "It looks like rain today" or "That car is yellow." The coach will say these statements to the trainee. The trainee will acknowledge each statement, every time, with a word and tone of voice to indicate they were aware and heard the statement, such as "Okay" or "Good" or "I got that, thank you."

The goal is to remain non-reactive yet present and to communicate the reception of the information. The goal is not to offer any evaluation of the information received, only that the information was received. If the coach has the impression that the acknowledgement was said in a rote manner or without actually perceiving what was said, they will use the time out signal and stop the exercise. Then the coach will briefly indicate why they didn't feel acknowledged and begin again. Continue until the trainee and coach both agree that the trainee is consistently acknowledging the coach. Trade roles and begin again. Here are some questions to assist you in your exercise:

1. Were there any immediate difficulties settling into the exercise? What was the reaction most often elicited?

2. Did any other emotions arise? As you think about them now, to what part of your map are they related? What was the trigger?

3. What was the difference you noticed between rote response and true acknowledgment? Did you have to agree to acknowledge?

EXERCISE 10: EMBARRASSMENT

This exercise ups the ante just a little. In this exercise, one partner will pick a slightly embarrassing story to reveal to the other partner. The goal for both partners is to remain non-anxious during the telling of the story. The partner who is hearing the story should not forget to acknowledge the other person, whenever appropriate. You will notice that both partners tend to become very reactive during the telling of the story. Each of you should attend to the reasons for your own reactivity. And each of you should attend to your most immediate urge to respond and/or do something.

The task for the storyteller will be to tell the story without changing it. This is often a huge task because it calls for managing feelings of guilt or shame without doing anything about them except simply allowing them to flow through you. Be curious. Notice how feelings of low self-esteem are triggered. Notice how often you evaluate yourself as bad, stupid, clumsy or whatever. And notice how often you assume the other person is thinking the same things. Notice the urge to do something to avoid the feelings. What did you have the urge to do? Find your one-point and relax. You don't have to do anything except stay in the non-anxious present. How are these feelings related to things you might have experienced from ages zero to eighteen?

The partner who listens to the story will also probably find the task a little unsettling. You will be triggered to react because of your own ego-states with low self-esteem. Notice your own feelings and urges to do something. How are these related to your own experiences from ages zero to eighteen?

Spend a very short time (five minutes or less) each debriefing the first part of the exercise. Try to stay non-anxiously in the here and now. Do not discuss the story or its content; discuss only your reactivity to the story. Try to put words to your experience of being triggered and what your urge to do might have been. Identify the ego-state and discuss earlier experiences when that ego-state was triggered and what you did when it emerged. Stay away from story content and stick with internal reactivity. Repeat the process with the same story teller and same listener until reactivity is at a minimum. Switch roles and begin again. Here are some questions to assist you with this exercise:

1. Were there any immediate difficulties settling into the exercise? What was the reaction most often elicited?

2. Did any other emotions arise? As you think about them now, to what part of your map are they related? What was the trigger?

3. What was the difference you noticed in your comfort with yourself as you related the story? Did this change your behavior?

4. What was the difference you noticed in your comfort with yourself and your partner as you heard the story? Did this change your behavior?

EXERCISE 11: COMPLIMENTS

This exercise is short and not so simple. One of you will look in the eyes of the other in a soft, relaxed manner and compliment them on something you have noticed about them in the previous exercises. Focus on only one aspect to compliment as you do the exercise. The person being complimented will use the acknowledging exercise. Both people should be curious about their reactivity.

Notice what comes up. For the person receiving the compliment, what self-talk are you using when you hear it? How is that related to your map? What effect does this reaction have on your behaviors in the here and now? Do you feel like you now owe the other person a return compliment?

There are a couple of facets to this exercise that are worth exploring. Our own self-talk often prevents us from hearing genuine compliments about who we are. We quickly negate or down play what we heard and thereby miss an honest appreciation of ourselves. This is partly because of our own low self-esteem and partly because we have become accustomed to hearing false praise from others with an agenda. The goal is to be able to hear comments about ourselves and then properly evaluate them internally to determine if they meet with our own expectations of our behaviors.

The feedback from others is just one piece of information we can use to determine whether our own intended behaviors and communications were successful. Are we presenting ourselves in one way and being perceived in another? However, this is only one piece of information. Again the question, why would you or should you take upon yourself someone else's evaluation of you even when it is positive?

In some cases, no matter what you do, you will be perceived differently than you expect. This is because the other person is viewing you through the filter of his or her own map. When you are self-validated, you can be gracious for the compliment and evaluate it against your own expectations of your behavior. There is no need to react in any other manner.

As the person giving the compliment, do you feel uncomfortable commenting on the other person? Do you feel phony when you say it? Does it feel like the comment is pulled from you without freely giving it? How is this related to your own experiences with compliments? Our maps have often taught us that compliments are rarely without strings. So, even when we give them we are semiconscious of the expectations of return.

These are not just social graces. These are driven by our social fears of being rejected and/or evaluated. The question you can ask yourself is can I give or receive a compliment freely without expectation of return?

Switch roles and continue the exercise. Be sure and return to a non-anxious presence whenever necessary. Discuss your reaction. Here are some questions to assist you with this exercise:

1. Were there any immediate difficulties settling into the exercise? What was the reaction most often elicited?

2. Did any other emotions arise? As you think about them now, to what part of your map are they related? What was the trigger?

3. What was the difference you noticed in your comfort with yourself as you heard the comment? Did this change your behavior?

4. What was the difference you noticed in your comfort with yourself and your partner as you made the comment? Did this change your behavior?

EXERCISE 12: HONORING RITUAL

In the next series of exercises, it is significantly more difficult to maintain a non-anxious presence. This is because you will now begin to really explore your and your partner's maps and triggers. This is the territory we guard with our lives and where we become the most reactive. Therefore, it is important to remind each other of our commitment to grow and willingness to traverse the territory of connection safely.

For the remainder of the exercises, I highly recommend you begin and end your explorations with the following ritual. You may also find it a wonderful way to greet each other, either regularly, if you are mindful and it does not lose its significance, or for special occasions when it is important to remind yourself and your partner of your commitment to growth and safe exploration.

The ritual itself is actually a form of a traditional style of greeting others (namaskar) in the East. In India, for instance, one slightly bows one's head, brings the hands together to the heart as if in prayer, and says namaste (pronounced nah – mah – sthay), which roughly translated means "The divine within me honors the divine within you." Done in the context of these exercises, it becomes a means of focusing your energy and intent in the present, honoring the divine within your partner, and committing to explore with love and patience.

Sounds rather simple. You may be surprised at the emotion it evokes. The honoring ritual is presented here first as an exercise because of the power it has to generate reactivity within you. Often making and/or receiving a gesture of commitment and intentionality evokes significant emotions. Be curious about what comes up. Later, you may find the exercise helps you re-focus your commitment to each other and keeping each other safe.

Seat yourself comfortably before each other. Find your one-point and create a non-anxious presence. Become mindful of your body and your presence in the here and now. Become mindful of your partner. Take a moment to allow your heart to fill with love for your partner. Gaze softly into each other's eyes. Then each of you in turn perform the following: place your hand, palm inward, to your heart.

Now extend it out toward your partner as if offering them a gift from your heart. As you extend your hand, say, "I honor the divine within you. I will to listen to you with my heart. I will act toward you from my heart." The other person should acknowledge this act appropriately.

Take some time to go inward and reflect on your experience. Begin to discuss what comes up. You may find you have to relax your one-point several times. You may find yourself becoming tearful. This is not unusual. Explore whether they are tears of sadness, tears of joy, or both. What are you sad about? What are you happy about? How does this affect your expectations? Recognize how much trust is based on one's ability to be intentional.

If you get side tracked and/or angry, recognize that it is your own feelings of abandonment that arise. Use this greeting before beginning each of the next exercises. Here are some questions to assist you with this exercise:

1. Were there any immediate difficulties settling into the exercise? What was the reaction most often elicited?

2. Did any other emotions arise? As you think about them now, to what part of your map are they related? What was the trigger?

3. What was the difference you noticed in your comfort with yourself as you heard the comment? Did this change your behavior?

4. What was the difference you noticed in your comfort with yourself and your partner as you made the comment? Did this change your behavior?

EXERCISE 13: EXPLORING YOUR MAPS

This next exercise may be very difficult. It will take a considerable amount of time, so you should plan to take a day or two to complete it. In this exercise you will begin to explore each other's map. By now you each should have done the Exploring Your Map exercise from Exercise 5: Triggers: Exploring Your Map in the first section. Hopefully, you gained insight into some of the triggers for your ego-states. If you haven't done this exercise, you should do it now, individually. Once completed, review your answers and identify areas you seem to have particular problems with, especially those areas that seem to be triggered by your partner. You may continue this exercise with the whole list or you may wish to make a separate list of the questions you think would be most important for your partner to understand and know about. You may also wish to add areas of your own to the list. Your selection of questions should include those that will provide information to your partner to help them better understand how they may trigger certain ego-states of yours.

Remember, your partner is not to blame for triggering your ego-states. This is not about blame. It is about understanding process and how you came to have reactive ego-sates in the first place. Eventually your partner may choose to modify their behavior if they understand how it may trigger you. This is not a necessity however, since it is your responsibility to manage your own reactivity. Nonetheless, the information will help them understand if you do happen to become reactive.

When you have completed the preparatory work, find a comfortable place where you will not be disturbed for several hours. You will be combining several of the previous exercises as you do this one. The most important exercise both of you will do during this exercise is maintaining a non-anxious presence. Find your one-point and relax – again and again. This exercise structure may feel a little stilted at first. Try it this way before you change your approach. It is structured because of the tendency for partners to get side-tracked and not finish the exercise. Once you get into the habit of creating a safe place to speak of painful experiences you can un-structure it any way you like.

Begin the exercise with the Honoring Ritual. This will help establish a safe atmosphere for exploration and growth. One partner will ask the questions from the other's list and the other will answer. For each of the specific questions on the list, ask the following additional questions.

1. Do you have any emotional reaction to this information?

2. What beliefs about yourself arise because of this information?

3. Are there specific words or behaviors that remind you of this?

4. Is there anything else you would like to say about this area?

The role for the person asking the questions is to be a witness. As you receive each answer use the Acknowledgement Exercise. Acknowledge each communication with an appropriate response such as "Thank you" or "Okay." Do not add anything else! This is very important. It is not your function to judge, evaluate, commiserate, fix, make better, or, at this moment, offer solace to your partner. Your partner is likely to be experiencing a little or a lot of emotion. This is not a signal for you to do anything! Your goal is to be a witness. Find your one-point and relax.

One cautionary note: Do not imagine because you have heard your partner describe their map, you know what motivates them. The exploration you are witnessing is always a work in progress. There are many layers of understanding and multiple factors that determine any behavior. And be very aware of this:

If you use this exercise as a way of mining for weapons, you have just violated the trust of your partner!!

In other words, if you later comment on this information in an angry manner or use it against your partner as a means of belittling them, you have demonstrated that you are untrustworthy to keep their heart safe. This is the part about having a companion who knows the inner most pain of your heart and never, ever uses it against you. Your role is to be a non-reactive witness. Can you be trusted to keep your partner's heart safe from your anger no matter what?

The role for the person answering the questions is to provide information as honestly and straight forwardly as possible. At times this may be a very difficult task because of the emotions elicited by the questions. Find your one-point and relax. It is your job to manage your reactivity. Try and be as specific and in-depth as possible. Look for nuances and be curious. Do not expect a response from your partner other than acknowledgment. It is not their responsibility to take care of you at this point. You will be faced with issues of trust. How do you trust your partner will hear what you have to say and not use it against you?

This exercise has two goals. First, it is a way for one partner to learn how the other partner's heart was broken and how and why they came to protect it. It will help you begin to see each other as real people instead of a fantasy of who you imagine each other to be or who you want each other to be. And, it will help you have compassion. Once we learn of the pain another has felt, we begin to understand their behaviors in a new light. It begins to make sense. And we learn we do not have to interpret their behaviors as necessarily being about us. Second, it will allow one partner to begin to put words to their own map, helping them gain insight into their own motivations and, perhaps, recognize for the first time how often their behaviors are reactions to old (mis)perceptions. Remember to do the Honoring Ritual when you are done. Here are some questions to assist you with this exercise:

1. Were there any immediate difficulties settling into the exercise? What was the reaction most often elicited?

2. Did any other emotions arise? As you think about them now, to what part of your map are they related? What was the trigger?

3. What was the difference you noticed in your comfort with yourself as you began answering questions? Did this change your behavior?

4. What was the difference you noticed in your comfort with yourself and your partner as your partner answered the questions? Did this change your behavior?

EXERCISE 14: NEGOTIATING MADE EASY

The following is about how we negotiate how our relationships work. While it is written in the context of a couple's relationship, it is just as valid when negotiating other relationships as well. This would include how you get along with your boss and how you get along with friends. Change the word partner to boss and the strategy is the same. Only the motivations may change.

So, how do you want your relationship to look? Are there changes you would like to see in the manner in which you live with your partner? How important are these changes? Have you noticed what goes through your mind when you think about negotiating these changes? How fearful are you? What are you afraid of? Negotiating how you want your relationship to look is an easy task - if you stay self-validated and intentional. The minute you become reactive, the negotiation becomes an argument.

In its simplest form, a good negotiation looks like this:

The first person says, "This is what I would like in our relationship. . ."

The second person either says, "I am willing to do that"
or "I am not willing to do that" or
"I am willing to do part of that."

The first person says, "I can live with that" or
"I can't live with that."

If they can live with that, the negotiation has been completed successfully. If they can't live with that it means they aren't willing to stay in a relationship that looks like that. The second person has a question to answer: What am I willing to do to stay in this relationship? If they want to stay in the relationship, they will rethink their first response.

At first blush it seems rather manipulative. It's either my way or the highway. However, from the perspective of two self-validated and intentional individuals, this is not even slightly manipulative. It is only from the perspective of someone who is externally validated and reactive that this seems manipulative, because they hear an implied threat in the "I can live with that" or "I can't." It is seen as manipulative because of their fear of being rejected and/or being alone. Let's tease this apart a bit farther.

The stumbling blocks in negotiating come specifically from external validation, reactivity and/or a failure to live with integrity. To begin with, we often fear asking for what we want because we fear we will be seen as broken, bad, mean, evil, stupid or uncaring. (You aren't.) This is about our own low self-esteem and worry that we will be rejected if we talk about what is in our hearts. Relax your one-point. What do you want? You really get to ask for things to be the way you want them. How important to you is what you are asking for? In other words, what are you willing to do to get it? Are you willing to overcome the habitual fear of rejection that usually prevents you from talking about your desires? Asking for what you want is the only way you will get it. We often have this fantasy that our partner should know what we want. (They don't.) And since they aren't giving it to us, they must be broken, bad, mean, evil, stupid or uncaring. (They aren't.) In a relationship, it is your responsibility to explicitly state how you want it to look. Having a fantasy that the other person knows or should know what you want and then reacting when it doesn't happen is map stuff at its worst.

When the second person hears a request, they can have one of two responses. First, because of their own maps, they may assume that since the first person is asking them to change, it must mean it is because the first person thinks they are broken, bad, mean, evil, stupid or uncaring. (It doesn't.) They then get reactive (angry) and defend themselves rather than negotiate. They accuse the first person of being broken, bad, mean, evil, stupid or uncaring. Of course, the first person has to defend, so simple requests turn into huge arguments.

The second response is one in which the second person understands the first person to be stating a preference in how their relationship looks. They also understand that stating a preference does not in any way imply that either person is broken, bad, mean, evil, stupid or uncaring. It is just a preference. The importance of the preference will be established by whether or not each can live with the answer. Even if the second person does not want to or cannot (because of their own strength of preference) provide the change that is being asked for, it does not mean they are broken, bad, mean, evil, stupid or uncaring. It may mean a change in relationship, but it does not mean either person is broken, bad, mean, evil, stupid or uncaring.

Remember when two people enter a relationship, they do so because they want to be in it, not because they have to be in it. Both individuals are invested in the relationship. It is a choice. And they get to mutually create their relationship to look the way they want it to look. This is done by negotiating, not by assuming. Each negotiation is a balance between the desire to be in the relationship and a desire to have their life look a certain way. There will always be negotiated compromise. It is the case that, for any decision we make, there are always consequences. Some we like and some we don't. Each person gets to balance the consequences of their decisions in a manner that suits them best. What they decide is not a matter of them or the other person being broken, bad, mean, evil, stupid or uncaring.

The most common error couples make when negotiating is believing preferences are about love. Your inner dialogue says, "If you loved me enough, you would give me what I want." Your partner could just as easily say, "If you loved me enough, you wouldn't ask for this." The issue is not about love. It is about deciding what is best for each person and how they want to live their life. It is a preference of lifestyles, not a comment on the other person's worth, the value of their preferences or the strength of their love. And this is true whether the issue is about who does the dishes or what sexual position or behavior you prefer.

Some preferences are so strong they are deal breakers. In other words, one person will refuse to be in a relationship that looks a certain way. It is perfectly acceptable to have preferences that strong. And each person will have to live with the consequences of the strength of their preferences. In this instance, not being with the other person.

This probably strikes an abrasive chord with those who think marriage is for better or worse, no matter what. However, many people get married before they are able to make good decisions about the person with whom they will spend the rest of their life. Because of their attachment addiction and need for external validation, they make less than useful choices. Sometimes they marry someone who, because of their own map, has a difficult time living with another person in a healthy manner and refuses to grow to become healthier. Under these circumstances, the first person has a difficult decision to make. Can I live with this or not? It does not necessarily mean they will leave the relationship. It just means the healthier person will have to live with more reactivity and need for external validation from the other person.

Integrity is also a big factor when you begin to negotiate. Do you say what you mean, mean what you say, and (this is the big one) do what you say you are going to do? If you agree to perform a certain behavior, do you follow through with it or not? If you do not, or fail to make an effort, you have demonstrated that you are not living with integrity. Under that circumstance, your partner has a decision to make. When you enter into a negotiation, do so with the expectation that you will live up to your commitments. If you do not live with integrity, you may be looking for a new relationship.

Now for the hard part. This will be an exercise in negotiating change. For this exercise, do not barter. The form of this negotiation considers only one request at a time. It should not be one in which one person requests a change and the other says, "I'll do this, if you'll do that." This is a more complex negotiation often loaded with hidden messages of either person being broken, bad, mean, evil, stupid or uncaring. Until you have more experience being a self-validated, intentional negotiator, stick with this simple form.

Each of you should take some time to think about how you would like your relationship to look. Make a list of the things you would like to change. Work your way through the list thinking about how important each change is. Try and include changes that are only marginally important, those that are more important, and those that are very important. Prioritize the list from least important to most important. For this exercise you will begin by using changes that are marginally important.

Keep this in mind. There are some things you might ask for that you will never get. You might ask a person to believe a certain thing, feel a certain way, think a certain way, or want a certain thing. If you ask for these things, you will be disappointed. They do not change by asking for them or even necessarily by intention. They change through experience. However, you can ask for any specific behavior you want or do not want performed. You may or may not get it depending on the strength of your partner's preference, but you can ask for any behavior.

Now summon up all the things you have learned from the previous exercises. Sit close enough to each other to be able to talk quietly. Relax your one-point. Do the honoring ritual. The first person will take the first item on their list and say, "This is what I would like to change in our relationship." It is your task to remain self-validated and intentional. Notice whether or not you are triggered simply by requesting a change. Relax your one-point. Just be curious. How important is this change to you. Are you prepared to live with the response?

The second person will consider the request. You should also remain self-validated and intentional. Notice whether or not you are triggered by having a change requested. Relax your one-point. Be curious. How important is the change to you? Are you willing to make the change, part of the change, or none of the change? Respond to the request. Remember, if you agree to the request you have to say what you mean, mean what you say, and do what you say you're going to do. Don't say you will when you won't. If your tendency is to say "yes" even when you don't want to do it, you are being reactive. Be curious about that.

The first person now has a decision to make. Can you live with this response or not? Since this is a small request you may be willing to live with whatever the response is. However, if it is not the response you wanted, it will certainly create reactivity. Be curious about your reactivity. Notice your tendency to think one or the other of you is broken, bad, mean, evil, stupid, or uncaring. Is that really the truth?

At this point, stop the negotiation. Do the Honoring Ritual. Take some time to discuss your internal responses with each other. Put words to your tendency to drop into external validation and reactivity. See if you can relate it to experiences from your past. As you put words to the experience, relax your one-point. If you find that you cannot manage your reactivity, stop the exercise. You have work to do. When you think you're ready, begin again. Continue with the exercise. As your changes become more important you will trigger more fearful ego-states. The likelihood that you will get reactive will increase unless you really managed to be intentional. Continue to be curious. Continue to discuss each negotiation, putting words to your own internal experience. Relax your one-point. When you think you are ready, work your way through the more important parts of your lists.

If you or your partner becomes reactive, stop the exercise. Do the Honoring Ritual with very focused intent. The partner that has become reactive probably has some work to do exploring their map and working on their self-validation and intentionality. Begin the exercises in Part One again. Be kind and gentle with yourself and explore with curiosity. Find the point where you get stuck and work the exercises. Then begin the couple's exercises again from the beginning. Here are some questions to assist you with this exercise:

1. Were there any immediate difficulties settling into the exercise? What was the reaction most often elicited?

2. Did any other emotions arise? As you think about them now, to what part of your map are they related? What was the trigger?

3. What was the difference you noticed in your comfort with yourself as you began the negotiation? Did this change your behavior?

4. What was the difference you noticed in your comfort with yourself and your partner as your partner answered? Did this change your behavior?

EXERCISE 15: THE HEART-SPACE - ALL OF ME

This exercise is new to ALOTH and truly delightful. It was created by Diana and Richard Daffner for use in their intimacy workshops[8] and they have graciously allowed me to use it in this book. Diana says it should be used whenever something is

---

8   Richard & Diana Daffner, C.S., M.A. can be contacted through www. IntimacyRetreats.com (941) 349-6804 (Toll free 1-877-282-4244). They have an amazing wealth of information and experience. Their workshops are wonderful opportunities to learn and experience how to play in intimate ways and practice the principles addressed in *A Language of the Heart*.

separating you from the experience of Love! Notice the capital letter "L."

While reading ALOTH and doing the exercises, you may have wondered where the concept of love comes into play. To remind you from the beginning of Part Two: love is "a many splendored thing," and, as it turns out, not very pertinent to good relationships. How often do couples report they "love" each other and can't stand to be in the same room together? This is because the word love means different things to different people even when they think they're talking about the same thing. The emotional experience of love is intimately tied to our emotional learning as children and is, therefore, part of our map. The exact experience that constitutes "love" for one person is different for another. Attachment addiction, excitement, romance, sexual attraction, deep emotional attachment, and wish fulfillment are all mixed to varying degrees in the reality of the definition of "love" for each person. And while it is certainly useful for each person to become curious about what the word "love" means to them specifically and determine to what degree that interpretation influences their relationship behaviors, these various components are all "self" oriented. In other words, they are about what the other person can do for "me." This doesn't mean that some of these components are not important. They just do not capture the true nature of the "Love" we seek.

The "Love" we all yearn for is not about that. It is about being accepted unconditionally for who we are. It is about the experience of being "seen" for who we really are, respected for our individuality and cherished for our "self." It is a gift given to us by another with no strings attached no expectations that we do anything in return. In other words, love is free. If we "love" someone and do things for them hoping they will "love" us in return, it isn't "Love." It's marketing! I'll give you this if you give me that. This is not unconditional. It is a trade with conditions attached. Herein lays the difficulty. And a paradox of sorts. To love someone you have to give up the need to be loved in return! No strings. It is an experience where you open your heart to the person you are with and make room for all of who they are. This is an experience in which you think to yourself and possibly say to another, "I delight in your existence." The thought of the fact they are in the world makes you happy. You send them spiritual energy from your heart that envelopes them and wants for them whatever will help them grow, even if it isn't you. This is truly what you have been wanting your whole life. The question is, "Can you give it to another – for free?"

The Heart Space – All of Me exercise is particularly powerful. It can be used both on an individual and personal basis (i.e. for your own benefit and personal acceptance of self) as well as with couples (i.e. for the benefit of your relationship). It is a wonderful opportunity to connect with all of your ego-states and those of your partners, even the ones that have been less than useful in the past. You see, each of us desires to be seen completely and accepted for who we are, in other words, loved unconditionally. However, we all have ego-states that can be less than useful in attaining our goal of companionship and love.

It's helpful to remember that even these "less than useful"

ego-states were created in the service of protecting your heart and seeking to be loved as well. When you work to become self-validated and intentional they are less often the ones that cause you to be reactive. Nevertheless, they still exist and occasionally need attention. Richard and Diana have done a wonderful job of explaining how this works and included in their explanation is a powerful spiritual dimension only hinted at in previous exercises. So I think I will present the exercise in their words. You will immediately see how this translates into the new language you have learned so far. At various points I have commented (in italics) to emphasize certain points.

To quote Diana and Richard:

Within each of us lives a multitude of "parts," various fragmented aspects of ourselves. Some of these parts are familiar; others may show up as a surprise, each with its own belief system, its own way of reacting to the world. Sometimes we are aware of one part of ourselves arguing with another part, one part trying to reason with another. Sometimes one part of us is annoyed, embarrassed, ashamed or amazed at how another part of us thinks and acts.

Of course, we are more than the sum of these parts. At the core of our being, there is a true wholeness that can expand to embrace all of our parts. This core, our essential being, is itself linked to a universal field of energy which resonates in the vibration of all life. We can think of this as our Divine Self, a state of being that expresses itself as Love. When we allow this Love to be fully present in our hearts, in our bodies, in our consciousness…we feel complete, no longer fragmented, no longer pushed or pulled by different parts of ourselves. Staying in the present experience of Love, we can hold the various parts of ourselves with non-judgmental compassion. As we embrace the whole of ourselves, Love makes itself known.

Intimacy invites us to reveal our love for our Beloved and our delight in the relationship. Intimacy also invites us to reveal parts of ourselves that may feel unloving or unloved. When these parts are ignored or kept hidden, a barrier can develop, preventing deeper intimacy. The parts themselves can be thought of as having a life of their own.[9] They often want something for us, trying to protect us or benefit us in some way – although their strategy for doing so may seem to create the opposite effect, often sabotaging our higher intentions for ourselves and our relationship.

…This is, of course, a good description of ego-states and a great description of how they may wait in the wings to sabotage what we are really trying to accomplish. They may keep up a running commentary on what we are doing or what our partner's behavior means. The commentary is quite often negative and fearful, based on our past experiences of rejection and abandonment…

As partners on a conscious path, we can learn together to gently turn our hearts toward these troubled or troublesome parts. We can discover what it is they are wanting. Feeling safe to communicate, no longer forced to hide, or to scream for attention, these parts may actually lead us into an exquisite sense of wholeness, healing and even more love.

Acknowledging a normally unwelcome part of ourselves does not mean condoning the behavior of that part

---

9 For more on this theory, see Ann Weiser-Cornell at FocusingResources.com.

or agreeing with that part's point-of-view. We are simply saying "hello," acknowledging that the part exists, recognizing it as carrying one or more strands of our own precious life energy. When we gently turn toward that part, giving it our compassionate attention, we might find that it releases its hold on us, allows our fragmented energy to be enfolded back into our essential being.

...This is an important point. Acknowledging a part does not mean it gets to "drive our bus." And when a partner acknowledges one of our parts it does not mean we then have permission to let it do what it wants to do. It will always be our responsibility to keep the agreement we have made to keep our partner's heart safe from our anger – no matter what...

We often strengthen these parts by struggling against them or pushing them aside. In our not wanting to give voice or expression to them, we may keep them even more alive within us! What if we allowed ourselves to acknowledge all the parts of ourselves, whatever shows up, in the presence of our Beloved? Together, we can help one another hold a sacred, compassionate space in which "all of me" can be accepted in any moment. Doing so, we can create an intimacy of shared presence that nourishes our erotic relationship and brings us more deeply into loving wholeness.

...One reason these parts seem to become more powerful when we struggle against them is because their experience is characterized by deep sadness. If they are ignored, it's as if the injustice in their lives and the pain in their heart are being ignored. They have a deeply felt need to be "seen", to be heard and have their pain acknowledged...

Sometimes a part may show up when we least expect it. We may suddenly notice uncomfortable feelings or sensations in us that we don't express out loud. We may be with our partner yet notice a minor resistance, a small pulling back. There might be some unexpressed anger or fear or sadness.

This exercise, All of Me, creates a safe way in which to explore the experience of turning toward these normally unwelcome parts of ourselves from a shared heart of love. It can be used as a lead-in to sacred loving or at any time. If you practice when you feel happily connected, it will be easier to recall the exercise when something uncomfortable really does come up, whenever you notice something separating you from the full experience of love.

Decide together how long you will do the practice. If done daily, even a few minutes can be transformational. To begin, face each other fully and declare your loving presence to each other, saying, hearing and feeling each other say, "I am here." Create a shared "Heart-Space." Look into each other's eyes and maintain eye contact throughout the exercise.

...A shared Heart-Space is a somewhat new concept for readers of ALOTH, though it is relatively easy to experience. It is an opportunity for you and your partner to consciously make room in your heart for all of each other, in other words, to demonstrate and experience unconditional love. This is an opportunity to recognize and accept the knowledge that we all have parts that perform "less than useful" behaviors and that we all struggle sometimes to be as outwardly loving as we really want to be. Again, it is not condoning or accepting these "less than useful" behaviors. It is acknowledging the broken hearts of the parts that want to perform them. Over time, doing the exercise will create a sense of acceptance and trust where important and sensitive matters can be discussed in safety and love. I suggest you begin this way:

Sit or lay facing each other

Relax your one-point

Perform the Honoring Ritual

From Diana and Richard:

Acknowledge that you are consciously in the present by saying "I am here"…

Partner A: Take a moment to notice something you are aware of. It could be an emotion or a body sensation, whether pleasurable or not. It could be a sound you hear or a scent you notice. Something you see in the environment. Find ONE thing. Reveal it, report it to your partner as if you are noticing a part of you that is feeling or sensing something.

I'm noticing a part of me that feels (wants, doesn't want, hears, smells, sees…)

OR There's a part of me that feels (wants, doesn't want… etc.)

OR I'm sensing something in me that feels …

Some examples:

I'm noticing a part of me that is annoyed by the loud car horns outside.

There's a part of me that feels silly doing this practice.

A part of me is aware of the sweet smell of your perfume.

I'm aware of part of me thinking about work.

I'm noticing a part of me that is really angry right now.

After stating that you are noticing a part of you…, ask your partner:

Will you help hold all of me, including that part of me, here in our Heart-Space?

Partner B replies:

Yes, I will help hold all of you, including that part of you, here in our Heart-Space.

Partner A:

Thank you.

Reverse roles and practice back and forth for five or ten minutes or however long you decided. Then use the format whenever appropriate in your daily lives together.

NOTE: In a more advanced version of this practice, the partner is asked to repeat back or paraphrase the description of the partner's experience.

Examples:

Yes, I will help hold All of You here in our heart-space, including that part of you that is feeling so angry right now.

Yes, I will help hold All of You in our heart-space, including that part of you thinking of work right now.

End of Diana and Richard's material.

This seems like such a simple exercise. Yet it has the power to transform your relationship with yourself and with others. It is about learning to love who you are and learning to love your real partner, not just your fantasy of who you think they ought to be. It is about acknowledging that we all have broken hearted ego-states that perform less than useful behaviors when we aren't paying attention and giving them the attention that will begin to heal their (your) heart. It is an act of "true" Love.

As you do the exercise, notice how reactive parts become when you are asked to hold your partner's (or your own) ego-states that are hurtful or angry toward you. Notice how difficult it is to lay down your defenses for a brief second of unconditional acceptance. This occurs because you probably still work under the notion that acknowledging those ego-states means you accept their behavior, which is especially true if your partner's behaviors continue to be hurtful. This is an integrity issue and one you will eventually have to face. Nonetheless, even if you eventually decide to leave the relationship, you will still be able to acknowledge the broken heart of your partner that continues to fuel unwanted behaviors.

Do the exercise a few times. After each effort answer the questions that follow. For the first few times you are doing the exercise, increase the sensitivity and importance of what you bring up. In other words, notice and acknowledge parts that you have been fearful or embarrassed to bring up in the past. As usual, if either of you find yourself becoming reactive, stop the exercise and return to Part 1 exercises until you can manage your own reactivity. Here are some questions to help you with this exercise:

1. Were there any immediate difficulties settling

into the exercise? What was the reaction most often elicited?

2. Did any other emotions arise? As you think about them now, to what part of your map are they related? What was the trigger?

3. What was the difference you noticed in your comfort with yourself as you asked for a part to be accepted? Did this change your behavior?

4. What was the difference you noticed in your comfort with yourself as your partner answered? Did this change your behavior?

5. What was the difference you noticed in your comfort with yourself as your partner asked for a part to be accepted? Did this change your behavior?

POINTS TO REMEMBER

If you have read this far and actually done the exercises, you should have begun to notice important changes in the way you talk to yourself, your partner, and others. It is likely you are more self-validated, more intentional, and less likely to interpret others' words and behaviors as being about you. You should notice there is less upset in your life and fewer times when you become angry. Here is a summary of significant points for you to remember. If you are going to speak to yourself in habitual ways, make these the habits.

1) Is my one-point relaxed?

2) Is my one-point relaxed? (It's that important.)

3) Am I safe or am I chasing lions? (No lion, no stress. Be a zebra.)

4) Who's driving my bus? (Which ego-state has control and is that who I want driving?)

5) Am I self-validated? (Why would I or should I evaluate myself by another person's evaluation of me?)

6) Am I intentional? (Why would I or should I react to another person's reactivity?)

7) Am I curious? (If I or my partner is reactive, what might we perceive as abandoning?)

8) What do I really want? (Every decision has consequences. Some I like, some I don't.)

PARENTS AND CHILDREN

About now, those of you who are parents are saying, "Oh my. What am I doing to my own children?" And, frankly, what you are doing is recreating the map you learned. This doesn't mean you are broken, bad, mean, evil, stupid or uncaring. It only means that you tend to recreate what you learned, even though it is not particularly satisfying. Remember the example about learning to read? Before you could read, were you broken, bad, mean, evil, stupid or uncaring? No, you just didn't know how to read. Before you learn how to parent, are you broken, bad, mean, evil, stupid or uncaring? No, you just recreate your own map. Even if you were the perfect parent and could read your child's mind, you would not be able to prevent the attachment anxiety that comes with birth, which leads to many of the problems of external validation. However, there are many things you can do to assist them in becoming self-validated and intentional.

Besides blindly recreating their maps, parents tend to make a fundamental mistake in their parenting. Parents often confuse love and discipline. Because of their own maps, parents interpret their children's misbehavior as not loving them, not caring what they say, not respecting them or reminding them of their inadequacies as parents. The inner dialogue says, "If they just loved me enough to listen to me or pay attention to me" or "I am such a lousy parent." In other words, parents are often externally validated and reactive. The minute this occurs, the parent first feels abandoned, then becomes angry. Of course, when they become angry, they reactively do something to hurt their children. They yell. They hit. They make disparaging comments. Children quickly learn they will need to defend themselves by lying, hiding or becoming passive aggressive. This usually makes the parent angrier and the merry-go-round begins to spin.

Here is a comment that brings varied reactions from parents: Do you know there is never a time when you need to be angry with your children? Pay close attention to your reaction to that comment. When you get angry, you are interpreting their behavior as abandoning of you. Then, you invariably react in hurtful ways toward them. Your anger is always about your own feelings of abandonment and it is always abusive. The question is, "If you truly love your children, why would you ever want to hurt them?" It is your own abandonment issues and feelings that you will never be good enough to be a good parent that result in your anger. You may cover this up with comments like, "That's how my parents taught me respect" or "Sometimes, they need a good swat to get their attention" or "Children should be seen and not heard," etc. But underneath those comments is that little voice that says, "If they loved me, they would do what I asked them."

Here's the real truth. Your children have to love you. They are programmed to attach to you. Even if you beat them, they will love you. Children even return to parents who are quite abusive. They cannot abandon you unless you make it an absolute survival issue. Eventually, for their own self-survival, they will withdraw their love and respect. However, for the first years of their life, they are yours, unconditionally.

Just as it is an error to confuse love and preferences, so is it an error to confuse love and discipline. Their behaviors are not about whether they love you or not. Children are programmed to explore and become individuals. Their behavior is often a manifestation of this program. They are looking to see what the limits are — the limits of both their own abilities and of society.

Here is another narrative you might use to describe the situation. Your children have one job and one job only - to see what the boundaries are. They will use anything at their disposal, any trick in the book to see if the boundary is real, including saying things like, "I hate you," "I want to run away," "I want to hurt myself." As a parent, you have just one job - to set clear consistent boundaries that will teach them how to survive and succeed in society. Rather than getting angry and thinking of them as broken, bad, mean, evil, stupid or uncaring for just doing their job and checking the boundaries, honor their creativity in thinking up ways to move them. And don't move the boundaries!

As children grow, their boundaries and abilities will expand. If you give them clear boundaries and allow them to experience natural consequences without disrespecting them, disparaging them or hurting them, they will become self-reliant, self-disciplined, self-validated and intentional. You can be as strict as you want as long as you treat your children with respect and dignity. Just deliver consequences dispassionately, without any emotion.

The key is consistency. Children will push against boundaries to see if they are real. When you provide clear consistent boundaries with consequences that occur every time the boundary is crossed, your children will learn the boundary is real and quit pushing against it. When the boundaries you set are not consistent, your children will learn they should just keep pushing. You have, in fact, trained your children to keep pushing the limits. This is an issue of integrity. Do you say what you mean and mean what you say? If you do, you will not only be teaching your children what the boundaries are, but modeling integrity. Be self-validated, intentional, and act with integrity.

OTHER DIFFICULTIES CHANGING OUR MAPS

As a final note, there are several issues that make changing maps more difficult than those already discussed. First, it takes a certain amount of early experience with good enough care-taking for us to have a building block for adequate self-soothing. Some of us have a particularly difficult time learning to self-soothe because we either did not experience adequate care-taking as children or we came to associate a negative meaning to self-care. This is especially true for men. However, if the message we got as children was intense enough, it is also true of women.

"Grow up, you baby."

"Be a man."

"Get over it."

These result in a strong injunction against doing anything to take care of ourselves. We think we have to "gut it out." And we expect others to "gut it out," as well. There is confusion between the determination to overcome hardship and the ability to feel and express emotion. The two are not mutually exclusive. Believing they are stunts our emotional growth. We become inflexible and eventually may break down from the stress of it. It takes special effort to change these scripts.

Second, because we have not learned adequate ways to self-soothe, we may turn to alcohol, drugs, work, food, sex or some other addictive behavior to do it. All of these numb the senses and emotions. If you are doing the exercises in this book and numbing yourself at the same time, you are not likely to accomplish your goals. You have to be able to feel what comes up and process it with a clear head. If you are drunk or stoned or tired or over-sated, you will not be able to access the information necessary for you to identify ego-states, emotions, and beliefs that brought you here in the first place. If you think you might have an addiction to any of these things, seek help to overcome them. You can do this work at the same time as you seek help. Just remember to be straight while you are doing the work.

Third, without going into the argument of whether or not schizophrenia is a biological problem, there is a certain sub-set of individuals with this diagnosis who were, unfortunately, raised in such a rigid and abusive manner they were left help-less in the face of it. These people have had drilled into them the message they will never be able to adequately care for themselves. Their parents are seen as and usually described as overwhelmingly emotionally and/or physically danger-ous. The message they received as children was specifically (not implied) that they were inadequate. They incorporate this message into their personality so strongly it manifests as voices that tell them they are worthless. Some voices even tell them they should die. Working with these voices is particularly problematic because the person is convinced that if they go against the voices, they will be subject to all the wrath of their overwhelming parent as personified by whomever they attribute their voices to. In such cases, medications are helpful. An evaluation by a psychiatrist is very important.

Fourth, when individuals experience specific traumatic events (sexual abuse, severe physical or emotional abuse, death of parents, accidents, acts of terror, war, or crime, etc), there are more severe consequences than usual. These individuals may experience greater incidents of depression, anxiety, panic attacks and dissociation. These symptoms are directly related to their trauma history. It is likely there are rigid ego-states associated with these events that make it difficult to proceed with the work of becoming self-validated and intentional. Under these circumstances, it is necessary to do specific trauma recovery work in addition to the normal work of therapy. There are many useful techniques to help work through these issues. However, it is important to seek out therapists who are adequately trained to recognize and treat them.

A LANGUAGE OF THE HEART: LOVE IS THE WAY HOME

Learning a language of the heart and speaking it when you interact with yourself and others will change your life. You have learned a new narrative that helps you understand your own behaviors and informs you that you are not broken, bad, mean, evil, stupid or uncaring. You have learned a new narrative that explains why others do what they do without having to interpret their behavior as abandoning or rejecting of you. You do not have to believe they are broken, bad, mean, evil, stupid or uncaring just because they do not agree with you and/or because you do not think they love you. And you do not have to believe their reactions or responses are about you being broken, bad, mean, evil, stupid or uncaring. Unless you are in an abusive relationship, their reactions are not threatening. They are not lions. If you are in an abusive relationship, you have a decision to make, because you never, ever have to be abused. When this information begins to sink in, your view of the world and the manner in which you interact with it changes. The language you use when you talk to yourself about yourself changes. And the language you use to describe others' behaviors changes, as well.

Here's an example. Your boss just called a decision of yours into question. At first, because of your map, you interpret this as him/her calling you stupid. A sad and anxious ego-state is triggered (Dad/Mom used to imply that you were stupid). Previously, you would begin to perform whatever behaviors that ego-state had learned to feel better about yourself. Perhaps you would have become angry and stormed out. Perhaps you would have become passive aggressive and sabotaged an important negotiation. Now you realize this is a sad and anxious ego-state. You relax your one-point. You ask yourself, "Am I safe?" Of course you are. You realize this is about Dad/Mom sadness. You allow yourself to acknowledge your sadness. Maybe you say to yourself, "Oh, there's that Dad/Mom stuff again." You realize this is neither about the boss calling you stupid, nor is it necessarily about you at all. Maybe the boss is having a bad day. Why would you or should you take upon yourself your boss's bad day? You have compassion for his internal states of low self-esteem because you have seen your own. Maybe your boss has ego-states that are consistently not particularly kind and loving. If that is the case, you may have a decision to make. Do I want to work here or not? And you do not have to be angry about it. You do not have to fall into fight-or-flight survival mode. You do not have to attribute your boss's behavior to him being broken, bad, mean, evil, stupid or uncaring — just brokenhearted. Like you. In fact, you may find yourself being curious about yourself and about your boss.

It is the same when you talk to loved ones. If you find yourself angry, it is because you are interpreting another's behavior as abandoning. An ego-state was triggered. Down the road you go.

Change the language, change the response. You will find that you have begun to think about yourself and them in a different way. You will recognize when ego-states are triggered and you will make every effort to care for them (your ego-states) in a loving manner. You will begin to care for others, as well. You will begin to relate to them with compassion, respect, dignity and kindness, because you will recognize the source of their reactivity is a broken heart. By not reacting in anger, you will demonstrate that you can be trusted. When you speak from the heart with love, you can be trusted. Others will begin to respond to you in a different manner. Your life and theirs will change. Speak a language of the heart.

Love is the way home.

APPENDIX A

THE ELEPHANT

The Parable of the Blind Men and the Elephant
(The original version from the Buddhist canon)

A number of disciples went to the Buddha and said, "Sir, there are living here in Savatthi many wandering hermits and scholars who indulge in constant dispute, some saying that the world is infinite and eternal and others that it is finite and not eternal, some saying that the soul dies with the body and others that it lives on forever, and so forth. What, Sir, would you say concerning them?"

The Buddha answered, "Once upon a time there was a certain raja who called to his servant and said, 'Come, good fellow, go and gather together in one place all the men of Savatthi who were born blind . . . and show them an elephant.' 'Very good, sire,' replied the servant, and he did as he was told. He said to the blind men assembled there, 'Here is an elephant,' and to one man he presented the head of the elephant, to another its ears, to another a tusk, to another the trunk, the foot, back, tail, and tuft of the tail, saying to each one that that was the elephant.

"When the blind men had felt the elephant, the raja went to each of them and said to each, 'Well, blind man, have you seen the elephant? Tell me, what sort of thing is an elephant?'

"Thereupon the men who were presented with the head answered, 'Sire, an elephant is like a pot.' And the men who had observed the ear replied, 'An elephant is like a winnowing basket.' Those who had been presented with a tusk said it was a ploughshare. Those who knew only the trunk said it was a plough; others said the body was a granary; the foot, a pillar; the back, a mortar; the tail, a pestle; the tuft of the tail, a brush.

"Then they began to quarrel, shouting, 'Yes it is!' 'No, it is not!' 'An elephant is not that!' 'Yes, it's like that!' and so on, till they came to blows over the matter.

"Brethren, the raja was delighted with the scene."

"Just so are these preachers and scholars holding various views blind and unseeing. . . . In their ignorance they are by nature quarrelsome, wrangling, and disputatious, each maintaining reality is thus and thus."

Then the Exalted One rendered this meaning by uttering this verse of uplift:

> O how they cling and wrangle, some who claim
> For preacher and monk the honored name!
> For, quarreling, each to his view they cling.
> Such folk see only one side of a thing.

—Udana 68-69

APPENDIX B
The Bus Driver Card

What do I really want?

Is that really the Truth about me?

What are my goals, right this second?

How does this remind me of things I might
have learned about myself from zero to eighteen?

What just occurred that elicited this state?

What am I feeling, right this moment?

— FOLD —

Who's driving this bus?

APPENDIX C

Exploring Your Map

The Exploring Your Map Exercise contains questions about different areas of your early experience. The list of questions is not exhaustive. For each question about an area of experience, ask yourself the following questions as well. Let me re-emphasize: The answers to the six immediately following questions are more important than any given answer to the long questionnaire.

What impact did these events have on your way of life, your outlook, your self-image, your sense of safety, your expectations, and your relationships with others?

To what degree would you consider the impact to be positive or negative? How so?

What are the beliefs about yourself that arose because of these events that you might question now?

What are the feelings the answers evoke and how do these relate to your current experience of the world.

**What are the exact words you used to help you organize
and understand the events they relate to.**

**What are the exact triggers that remind you
of these events?**

Your answers will help you understand how you came to see
yourself and understand relationships the way you do.

1) Are there family myths surrounding your birth and early
   childhood (e.g., words describing you as a difficult birth,
   intentional/unintentional pregnancy, wrong gender,
   cranky temperament, beautiful baby, smart, slow, etc)?

2) What are the exact words used to describe you as an in-
   fant, child, teen?

3) What were the circumstances of your care giving (e.g.,
   breast/bottle fed, daycare, parents worked)?

4) How many siblings did you have and what was your
   birth order?

5) Were you adopted, raised by others than your parents, or
   did you live in foster care for any length of time?

6) Did either parent pass away while you were growing up?

7) What, if any, significant events occurred during the first
   five years, 5 to 10 years, 10 to 18 years of your life (family moved, went to hospital, went on vacation, death of
   someone close)?

8) What are your earliest memories? Are they pleasant or
   not so pleasant? Which stand out the most?

9) How would you describe your emotional interactions with each parent, each sibling as an infant/toddler, primary/secondary school, teen, adult?

10) Were there conflicts with any of the people in the above questions? How were they managed?

11) What are some of the exact words used in your communications with each in the above two questions?

12) With whom were you closest? Why?

13) With whom were you the most distant? Why?

14) Were you treated with respect and dignity? If not, who did not?

15) Was anyone psychologically intrusive as you were growing up (head games, double messages, your feelings used against you, felt like you were not safe in your own mind)?

16) What is your current relationship with the above persons?

17) How did your parents discipline you? Under what circumstances?

18) What were your responsibilities as a child (chores, taking care of siblings, etc.)?

19) Were you ever left alone for periods of time?

20) Were you ever frightened? What caused it? How did you and others respond to your fright?

21) Were you ever in serious trouble at home, school, elsewhere? What were the circumstances? Outcomes?

22) What were your friends like? Were they allowed to visit you in your home? Why or why not? How did your parents interact with your friends?

23) Did your peers ever make fun of you or treat you in a disrespectful manner?

24) How would you characterize the emotional atmosphere of your home (warm, tense, edgy, quiet, calm)?

25) What were holidays like? Birthdays?

26) How were gifts given in your childhood? Were there strings attached?

27) How and from whom did you receive recognition?

28) Were your parents ever divorced? More than once? With whom did you live?

29) Did you have step-parents? What was your relationship with them like?

30) Did either parent have a relationship with or live with a person to whom they were not married? What was your relationship with them like?

31) Did either parent have a previous family? What was your parents' relationship with that family like? What was your relationship with them like?

32) How did your parents communicate with each other?

33) Was there conflict? How did that look (e.g., passive, aggressive, violent, yelling, hitting, threatening)? Under what circumstances? What did you do when conflict occurred?

34) How did your parents demonstrate love to each other, your siblings, you, others? Under what circumstances? Were there favorites? How did that manifest?

35) Was either parent unfaithful? How did you know? What was the result?

36) Did your parents use alcohol or drugs? Was it a problem? How did it manifest?

37) Was either parent absent for long periods?

38) Were your parents outspokenly biased or prejudiced? How did that manifest?

39) Was either parent psychologically impaired? How so? Physically? How so?

40) Did you have physical or psychological problems? How were they addressed?

41) Would you consider either parent abusive (emotionally, physically, sexually)?

42) Have you experienced any form of abuse (emotional, physical, sexual) from family members or others?

43) Were you ever touched in a way that left you feeling uncomfortable?

44) Were you ever stared at or had comments made about your body, your development, or your looks in general?

45) When and how did you learn about sex?

46) When and how did you become sexually active?

47) Were you ever subjected to racist remarks or prejudice?

48) Were comments ever made about your intelligence or your abilities?

49) What were your experiences in school?

50) Did you have learning difficulties? If so, how did family and/or others respond to your difficulties?

51) What was your socio-economic status?

52) Were you raised in a rural, small town, suburban, urban, or mixed community?

53) Did you work for money as a child? What were the circumstances?

54) What did you do for fun (activities: scouting, church groups, athletics, other)?

55) What was your weight and body build? Was it a problem?

56) Where you anorexic/bulimic, other?

57) Were you athletic?

58) Did your parents participate in outside activities with you? How was that experience?

59) What was your experience leaving home? Were you relieved, sad, anxious, excited?

60) Are there other areas not asked about in these questions that were a problem for you?

APPENDIX D
Recommended Authors

CONFLICT RESOLUTION:

Sheila Heen, Douglas Stone, Bruce Patton - Authors of *Difficult Conversations*; www.triadcgi.com

PARENTING SKILLS:

Jane Nelson - Co-Author of *Raising Self-reliant Children in a Self-indulgent World*; www.positivediscipline.com/jane.html

John Rosemond - Author of *Parent Power*; www.rosemond.com

PERSONAL AND SPIRITUAL GROWTH:

Don Miguel Ruiz- Author of T*he Four Agreements and The Mastery of Love*; www.miguelruiz.com

Neale Donald Walsch- Author of *Conversations with God - Books 1, 2 and 3*; www.cwg.org

Susan Anderson - Author of *The Journey from Abandonment to Healing*; www.abandonment.net

Gary Zukav - Author of *The Seat of the Soul*; www.zukav.com/welcome.html

Dan Millman - Author of T*he Way of the Peaceful Warrior*; www.danmillman.com/welcome.html

Drunvalo Melchizedeck - Author of *The Flower of Life: Volumes 1 and 2*; www.drunvalo.net

Dr. Masaru Emoto - Author of *The Hidden Messages in Water*; www.hado.net

Dr. Bruce Lipton - Author of *The Biology of Belief - Unleashing the Power of Consciousness, Matter and Miracles*; www.brucelipton.com

William Arntz, et. al. - Authors of *What the (Bleep) Do We Know*; www.whatthebleep.com

Dr. Richard Bartlett – Author of *Matrix Energetics and The Physics of Miracles*; www.matrixenergetics.com

Chogyam Trungpa Rinpoche – Author of *The Sacred Path of the Warrior*; www.Shambhala.com/chogyamtrungpa

INTIMACY:

Margot Anand - Author of *The Art of Sexual Ecstasy*; www.margotanand.com

David Schnarch - Author of *Constructing the Sexual Crucible and Passionate Marriage*; www.passionatemarriage.com

STRESS:

Thich Nhat Hahn - Author of *The Miracle of Mindfulness*; www.plumvillage.org

Robert Sapolsky - Author of *Why Zebras Don't Get Ulcers*; med.stanford.edu/profiles/Robert_Sapolsky/

FICTION:

Deepak Chopra - Author of *The Daughters of Joy: An Adventure of the Heart*; www.chopra.com

Italo Calvino – Author of *CosmiComics;* des.emory.edu/mfp/calvino

ABOUT THE AUTHOR

Dr. D. Franklin Schultz is a clinical psychologist in private practice in Lakeland, Florida, and is licensed in both Texas and Florida. He has been providing therapy in both in- and out-patient settings since 1984 and has been licensed as a clinical psychologist since 1994. Dr. Schultz is the author of *A Language of the Heart: Therapy Stories That Heal, A Language of the Heart Workbook* and co-author of a cognitive behavioral treatment book: *Trauma Practice: Tools for Stabilization and Recovery and workbook: Tools for Trauma: A CBT Approach.* He is a Master Traumatologist and certified compassion fatigue specialist. Since 2007, Dr. Schultz has been presenting *A Language of the Heart* as a workshop for individuals and couples. The principles of *A Language of the Heart* are also being used in business oriented workshops. You can contact Dr. Schultz at drfrank@aloth.com or go to the website www.aloth.com for more information.

CPSIA information can be obtained
at www.ICGtesting.com
Printed in the USA
LVOW08s2132080317
526559LV00001B/62/P

9 781614 934936